Write
to Sell

About the author

Andy Maslen graduated in Psychology and Anthropology from Durham University, in England. He then started work, as a sales representative for a DIY products importer. He also worked as a cook in an Italian restaurant.

In 1986, he began his marketing career, promoting business reports, journals and directories through direct mail. After ten years working in the corporate sector, including a six-year stint as a marketing director, he set up Sunfish, his copywriting agency, in 1996.

Today, he is one of the UK's leading independent copywriters, helping organizations of all sizes build sales and profits through the written word—both online and offline.

Andy is a Fellow of the Institute of Direct Marketing. He writes and speaks regularly on copywriting and co-founded *Write for Results*, a business writing training company. He also publishes *Maslen on Marketing*—a free monthly e-zine.

Andy is also the author of *100 Great Copywriting Ideas: from leading companies around the world* and *The Copywriting Sourcebook — How to Write Better Copy, Faster for Everything from Ads to Websites*, both published by Marshall Cavendish.

Find out more at www.andymaslen.com.

Andy Maslen

Write
to Sell

The ultimate guide to great copywriting

NEW EDITION

Marshall Cavendish
Business

For Jo, Rory and Jacob, with Love

Copyright © 2009 Andy Maslen
First published in 2007
This edition published in 2009, reprintd 2013 by
Marshall Cavendish Business
An imprint of Marshall Cavendish International

1 New Industrial Road, Singapore 536196
genrefsales@marshallcavendish.com
www.marshallcavendish.com/genref

Other Marshall Cavendish offices: Marshall Cavendish International (Asia) Private Limited, 1 New Industrial Road, Singapore 536196 • Marshall Cavendish Corporation, 99 White Plains Road, Tarrytown, NY 10591 • Marshall Cavendish International (Thailand) Co Ltd. 253 Asoke, 12th Flr, Sukhumvit 21 Road, Klongtoey Nua, Wattana, Bangkok 10110, Thailand • Marshall Cavendish (Malaysia) Sdn Bhd, Times Subang, Lot 46, Subang Hi-Tech Industrial Park, Batu Tiga, 40000 Shah Alam, Selangor Darul Ehsan, Malaysia

Marshall Cavendish is a trademark of Times Publishing Limited

The right of Andy Maslen to be identified as the authors of this work has been asserted by them in accordance with the Copyright, Designs and Patents Act 1988.

ISBN 978-0-462-09975-0

Designed by Rick Sellars
Data manipulation by Phoenix Photosetting Limited

Printed and bound by CPI Group (UK) Ltd, Croydon, CR0 4YY

Contents

A note

Throughout this book I use the word "selling". Please accept that I use this term in its widest possible meaning. That is, persuading someone to do or feel or think something they don't start off doing, feeling or thinking.

As well as the classic sales goals of winning orders or generating leads, it could mean influencing an internal committee to allocate budget to you or your team; getting a pay rise or a promotion; securing a new agreement with a distributor; or even gaining preferential treatment from a hotel.

Introduction

Writing clearly in English—the standard language of the Internet, not to mention business—has never been more important.

Just think of all the times you put fingers to keyboard. Letters, reports, proposals, publicity and marketing materials, emails . . . the list is long. If you can write well, you are more likely than the next person to get what you want.

As a professional copywriter and writing coach, I see a lot of copywriting. And much of it is mediocre at best.

Too often, copywriters achieve their goals not because of what they write but despite it. With this in mind, I set out to write a simple guide to good copywriting.

My aims are to:

- Help you write better sales copy, faster.
- Inspire and entertain you along the way— writing should be fun, too.
- Share with you some of the professional secrets I've learned over the past 20 years.
- Show you that it's not as hard as you might think to write well (though it does take practice).
- Give you a copywriter's toolkit stuffed with practical hints, tips and techniques for better copywriting.

Overall, to:

- Help you get results using the written word.

I know you're busy. And I know that you don't want to have to plough through a dense textbook. That's why this book is short. But don't be misled by its size. I've packed enough ideas between its covers to transform the way you write. I'll help you answer the really big questions facing every copywriter:

"How do I persuade someone to buy from me using nothing but the written word?"

"What does good copywriting look like— and sound like?"

"How can someone who isn't a professional writer still write compelling, persuasive, believable sales copy?"

"How do design and layout affect the impact of my writing?"

Four things you MUST remember about copywriting

1   Copywriting is about selling

There are lots of people out there who need to write sales copy but who aren't equipped or trained to do it well. They are doing it badly because they have never been shown how to do it properly.

Yes, people are taught to write at school (sometimes even quite well). But there is a deep chasm between academic writing and effective copywriting.

Why? Because copywriting is primarily about selling and only secondarily about writing. And that distinction calls for an understanding of people and what makes them tick. Yes, of course you need to be able to write well and correctly, but that alone will not take you all the way.

I'm often asked whether my degree is in English. It's not: I read psychology. If you are going to influence people using the written word, it helps if you understand a little about how their minds work.

2   We must focus on the reader

Most copywriting underperforms because it is all about the writer and not about the reader.

Business owners are in love with the company. Managers are in love with the product. Agency copywriters, frequently, are in love with themselves (bound by their artistic aspirations and their desire to win creative awards doled out by their peers).

But who's in love with the reader? Who's trying to figure out what they want to hear? What their needs and wants are? What will motivate them to pay attention to a sales message, believe it and act upon it?

3   Beautiful things come in small packages

Most business copywriters, especially in-house copywriters, assume that bigger is better. Long words are better than short words. Long sentences are better than short sentences.

But readers—even CEOs—do not engage with this style of writing. It's all head, no heart. To engage our reader, we must use wheelbarrow language: the earthy, flinty words we can almost pick up in our hands and smell.

4   Most people lack the necessary skills and experience to do it well

Most copywriters have never done any selling. If they have, they've often missed the connection between the two activities. That means they don't see how their writing works as a sales process. They lack the relevant experience.

Most sales people have never done any serious writing, so they lack the relevant skills.

Ten ways this book helps you

This book:

1   Gives you insights into how to gain your reader's attention, respect and trust.

2   Gives you the confidence to try a new approach to copywriting.

3   Helps you understand the relationship between selling skills and copywriting skills.

4   Saves you time, effort and heartache when you next want to write sales copy.

5   Means you won't waste money on doomed sales and marketing communications.

6   Gives you practical, easy-to-use tools to craft better copy.

7   Frees you from anxiety about so-called "correct" English.

8   Shows you specific techniques for improving the readability of your copy.

9   Refreshes your knowledge of some basic rules of good written English.

10 Helps you to get sales, marketing and commercial results.

Getting what you want is what this book is all about. Its techniques and ideas are designed to help you with:

*   Letters—selling, enquiring, agreeing, informing, complaining.
*   Emails—to clients, colleagues, staff, managers, suppliers.

- Reports—for clients, colleagues, boards, regulators, investors.
- Proposals—to win funding, secure approval, generate new business, excite investors.
- Public relations—press releases, articles, newsletters.
- Marketing—advertisements, direct mail letters, leaflets, brochures, websites, emails.

In other words, this book is about goal-focused writing. In each of the above, you have a specific aim in mind. It could be anything from generating a simple sales enquiry to winning a multi-million pound contract. But to achieve it, you have to do something special.

You have to change someone's behaviour.

Through the power of your writing, you have to get someone to do what you want them to do. The reader is in one mind when they get up in the morning; they've changed it once they've read your copy.

How do we change someone's behaviour? *Write to Sell* will set you on the right path. We'll look at the copywriting process from start to finish—everything from understanding your reader to designing your text so they feel compelled to respond.

Section One

It's not about you

*"Writing, when properly managed
(as you may be sure I think mine is)
is but a different name for conversation."*

Laurence Sterne, English writer, 1713—1768

Chapter 1
Where most people go wrong

If this book is about any single thing, it's about understanding your reader. Not your product. Not your company. Not your current special offer or promotion.

Something I learned very early in my career as a copywriter was that the only person who counts is the reader. It doesn't matter what you think. It doesn't matter what your manager thinks. It only matters what your reader thinks (and feels). That means you have to do something that might feel strange at first. You have to write not what you want to write, but what your reader wants to read.

Many men still believe the "chat up line" is the route to a woman's heart. But pre-prepared lines usually fail. Why? Because they don't take into account the recipient's feelings—they're all about the sender.

Ditto for much copywriting. If the copywriter has a plan at all—and more on planning in Section Two—it generally involves a list of the points they want to make, the information they want to get across, the facts they want to write about. Much rarer, about as rare, in fact, as a four-day-old mayfly, is a plan focusing on the reader. On their wants, needs, expectations, ambitions.

But without taking our reader into consideration, we're heading for trouble. All we can do is talk about ourselves—and we know what happens to people like that at parties.

Why *you* have to work harder
There's a simple reason why you have to write for your reader—not yourself, not your boss, not your colleagues. And it has to do with the level of investment they make in your writing.

Imagine your reader sitting at their desk or in their sitting room at home. The post arrives and, after retrieving it, they return to their chair. After putting bills to one side they are left with three items:

1   A letter postmarked Australia—the handwritten address shows it's from their old friend Lydia.

2   That month's issue of *Gardening Today* magazine, complete with a free trial-size sachet of bonemeal fertilizer.

3   Your mailshot.

Your mailshot is the odd one out. It's the only one in which they have no investment. They haven't paid for it. They didn't seek it out. They don't care who wrote it.

When people have an investment in reading—either emotional or financial—they will read. And they'll read despite poor spelling, faulty grammar, loose punctuation, unengaging tone of voice or any one of the many insults it's possible to inflict on the English language. When they don't have that investment, they will be ruthlessly unforgiving.

The only thing that will get their attention and keep it is a message aimed squarely at them—their interests, their concerns, their lives. A message delivered in such effortlessly good English that they don't notice the writing, just the content.

Copywriter's toolkit: Radio WIIFM

Whenever you sit down to write—it doesn't matter what: a sales letter, press release, web page or email—first tune in to the frequency your readers are all transmitting on: Radio WIIFM.

What your reader wants to know, what every reader wants to know, is the answer to a very simple question. What's In It For Me?

Send your message on this frequency and you'll have a far better chance of being listened to. Send on WIII (What I'm Interested In) and you'll lose them to a more interesting station.

Chapter 2
A few thoughts on human nature

Did you know that men think about sex every six seconds? That means if you write a letter that takes four minutes to read, your carefully crafted sales pitch gets interrupted 40 times. I have no idea (a) where that statistic came from and (b) whether it's true (I suspect it's a teeny weeny bit of an exaggeration). However …

The depressing truth—for us as copywriters, anyway—is that on any given day, at any given moment, our reader is far likelier to be focusing on something they care about than our sales message. Here's my point. Being a good copywriter means knowing your product inside out and being able to write convincingly about it. Being a great copywriter means knowing your reader the same way—their foibles, their motivations, their innermost fears and desires.

Before we put finger to keyboard, we need to build a psychological profile of our reader. Here's a list of questions I like to ask about the typical reader when I'm writing some copy:

1   What sex are they?
2   How old are they?
3   What do they want more of (and less of) in their lives?
4   Where would they rather be right now?
5   What do they want more than anything else out of life?
6   What are their values?
7   How do they see themselves?
8   How do others see them?
9   Are they head or heart people?
10 Are they more likely to be tempted by the promise of riches or the removal of worry?

Why ask these questions? Because I am always aware of this section's opening point: my reader would rather be thinking about something else. The more insights I can gain into the reader's preferences, state of mind and general outlook on life, the easier I'll find it to write copy that speaks directly to them in a way they'll find hard to ignore.

Not everyone shares my view, of course. Here are three things that many copywriters imagine their prospective customers find interesting. I assume they do because so many sales letters, ads and emails begin like this. (I'm going to follow this list with some things that customers DO find interesting.)

What people are REALLY interested in

Things that many copywriters think their customers are interested in:

1 The copywriter's state of mind. Eg "I am delighted to tell you ..." or "We are pleased to announce ..."
2 Statements about the customer's job, industry or hobby. Eg "As a busy finance director, you need to know about ..." or "Recent years have witnessed an explosion of interest in building cathedrals out of used matchsticks."
3 Narratives explaining the copywriter's company's development (usually from humble roots) eg "We began publishing Practical Composting in 1979. Since then ..." or (and very common nowadays) "We have totally redesigned our website ..."

Now for that list of things people like reading about:

1 Themselves.
2 Er ...
3 That's it.

Now of course I don't mean that you, as a copywriter, should tell people about themselves. Apart from anything else, when you display the fruits of your list research or database analysis, you'll come across as a stalker. You know the kind of thing:

"Dear Mr Sample,
With your preference for red satin boxer shorts, you'll be dying
to get your hands on Sexy Beast, our new catalogue featuring
exotic underclothing for today's go-getting gentleman."

No, I mean, write about your product or service from your reader's perspective. Don't tell them what it is: tell them what it does for them. In fact, I'll be more specific. Tell them how your product will make their life easier, better or more rewarding. If you don't know, find out, work it out or make something up. In other words, talk benefits (more about these in Chapter 5).

Love the sinner, then sell to them

If you don't feel like wearing your psychologist's hat, how about dusting down your theologian's gown?

Peel away the business suits, the carefully constructed personae, the intellectual body armour with which most people protect themselves from the truth, and you're left with humanity in the raw. And it turns out we're all sinners. So why not exploit the worst in human nature to achieve your goals?

Let's remind ourselves of the seven deadly sins and then look at how we might use them in our copy:

1   PRIDE (also known as vanity)—A simple way to make your reader believe you is to flatter them. Tell them how important they are. Acknowledge their huge knowledge and experience. They won't gainsay any of it. Then suggest that someone with their obvious talent for making the right decision really ought to be subscribing/buying/going along with your suggestion.

2   ENVY—Make them aware that other people already have the thing you're selling and are benefiting hugely as a result. Nobody likes to miss out and if they feel that the people with whom they identify are all having a great time enjoying product X, they'll want to join the party.

3   GLUTTONY—Why do people eat more than they need? Maybe they like the taste. Or the sensation. Maybe they're in need of comfort. Or solace. Unless you're selling food or promoting a restaurant, this sin won't have much relevance for you. BUT ... if your product makes people feel happy and contented when they 'consume' it, you have a real selling point.

4   LUST—A little harder, this one. But if you can suggest that becoming a customer of yours will satisfy this particular little craving, you're on to a winner. (I'd also suggest that you're wasted in your current job and should be on talk shows.)

5   ANGER—People get angry about all sorts of things. I had a problem with my ISP a couple of years ago that made my teeth grind like a pepper mill. Give people an exit route from this unpleasant emotion and they will thank you. If you know that your main competitor is making their customers angry (through failings such as poor service or product quality and excessive price rises), you have some great leverage to capture market share.

6   GREED—A major motivator for sales people through the ages. People sometimes want stuff they don't need. People often want more of what they've already got. Especially profits, pay, respect, office space, bottles of wine, pens, calculators, holidays, cars and clothes. Promise your customers MORE and you'll have their ear.

7   SLOTH—People are lazy. So show them how your product or service can save them energy. Perhaps they can sit at their desk and have stuff emailed straight to their desktop. Maybe you'll deliver something direct to their door instead of their having to walk to the shops. Help them avoid work and they'll open their wallets.

So remember …

Whether you are selling to consumers or people at work, ignore the baser human emotions at your peril. Yes, people will want to RATIONALIZE their decisions, so make sure you provide plenty of objective reasons why buying your products is a sensible thing to do. But people BUY on emotional grounds first. So make sure you hit at least one of the deadly sin buttons in your sales pitch. (By the way, only a beginner would tell their reader that they were lazy, lustful or greedy: BE SUBTLE.)

Chapter 3
Getting to know your reader

"But how do I know what my reader is like?" I hear you ask.

Simple. You have to think your way into their head. And their heart. What drives them? What motivates them? What excites them? These are the things you have to know before you start writing.

Understand your reader and you'll find it a lot easier to sell to them. Here's an example of how even a superficially simple mistake ruins the effect you're striving for.

I received a letter recently from my business bank. The name and address showing through the window of the envelope were fine. But when I scanned down to the start of the letter, what was the greeting? Not "Dear Mr Maslen", not, "Dear Andy", but "Dear Customer".

How can they get it so wrong? This is a covering letter from the head of business banking introducing the winter edition of their customer newsletter. So the whole point of the letter—the whole campaign—is to build rapport with their business banking clients. Is this a training issue? Does the author not know about mail-merging? More likely, they just couldn't be bothered to THINK.

Instead of feeling, "this bank knows me and cares about me", I thought, "more mass-produced garbage". And I would have thought that had I not been a professional copywriter.

What makes your reader tick?
Just as novelists have to understand their characters' inner lives, so business copywriters need to understand their readers in the same way. We must be able to call to mind their feelings, likes and dislikes, hopes and fears if we are to stand a chance of engaging their attention and getting the response we're looking for.

We need to remember that they are not just data on a mailing list or a demographic segment. They are living, breathing human beings with at least as many feelings as us. Because, after all, they are us. To paraphrase David Ogilvy, the founder of Ogilvy & Mather, one of the world's most successful advertising agencies, "the reader's not an idiot, he's your husband".

In my line of work, I have to be able to sell to widely varying groups of people (sometimes in the same week). Here are just some of the people I have had to get to know, understand and reach out to:

- Sleep-deprived, middle-class parents
- Professional historians
- Nursery nurses
- Corporate lawyers
- Grocers
- Lovers of Indian food
- Chief executives
- Human resources managers
- Lonely posh people
- Intellectuals
- Computer geeks
- Aspiring athletes
- Stressed head teachers
- Merchant bankers
- Small investors
- Sales and marketing directors
- Savvy 21st century women
- Road transport engineers
- Media studies students

In each case, before I worked out what to say to them, I had to get inside their heads. I had to figure out what they were looking for, what their pain was … and how to make it go away.

Copywriter's toolkit: The 3am question
If you want to zero in on the prime motivation driving your reader, ask them this simple question: "What keeps you awake at 3am?"

Your product may not be able to put them back to sleep, but you're missing a trick if you don't at the very least TRY.

And how do you find out?

How do you get your knowledge of your customers? Here are some channels many people rely on:

- Database reports
- Market research surveys
- Transcripts of focus groups
- Analysis from mailing or fulfilment houses
- What their advertising agencies tell them

Now, these are all very useful sources. IF you want to rely on second- or third-hand information. AND you only want aggregated data about your customers as a group. But what do they tell you about individual customers? About people? Here's what I suggest instead.

Get down to the engine room

I'm willing to bet you work in an office, cubicle or open-plan desk-desert. Any customers up there? I thought not. So, put your phone on divert, leave an "out of office" message on your email and go …

to one of your shops
to your call centre
to your customer service department
to an exhibition
to a conference
to a client's office

… and when you get there, start talking to your customers. (If you write for internal customers, find out where they work and go to meet them. That could be a factory, for example, or another department. DON'T rely on email.)

Observe them. Meet them. Speak to them. Figure out (or simply ask them) what they want from your products, your company, even you personally. Then, next time you sit down to write some copy to one of them, you'll have a HUGE advantage.

Now there are no more leaps of the imagination as you try to adopt the right tone of voice.

No more wondering if you're pressing the right buttons.

No more lacklustre letters filled with stuff your reader doesn't care about.

Instead, all you have to do is write down what you'd be saying to them if you were back in the shop, on the phone or at the trade show.

Keep it real

I recently finished the copy for a mailshot for a new women's magazine. My research was easy. I asked my wife and my other women friends to write the copy for me. (Well, OK, I did the keyboard bashing, but they told me what to write.)

And because these are real people, I could see them and hear how they talk. I know what they wear, how old they are, what their concerns are and what's likely to make them subscribe.

I also got to sit outside my favourite café in the Market Square with a cappuccino reading a pile of women's magazines and watching the girls go by (all in the name of empathizing with my reader, naturally).

Talk to your sales people

Sales people are one of your greatest resources as a copywriter. Unlike those of us who spend the greater part of our time chained to a desk, sales people (or the good ones, anyway) spend the greater part of theirs in front of clients.

So sales people KNOW what makes customers tick. Buy them a beer and they might even tell you. (And if you're a sales person, buy yourself a beer!)

Now maybe this sounds impractical or too time-consuming. Maybe you don't have sales people, or your customers all do business with you online. (Hey, ever heard of chatrooms?) But the more you know about your reader, the easier it is to write for them. And if you can't find out the answers, then you need to use another tool in the copywriter's toolkit. Your imagination.

Here's a story that shows you what I mean.

The PC magazine mailshot

One of my first freelance copywriting jobs was a mailshot for *Personal Computer World* magazine. I wanted to build a mental picture of the typical reader. So I talked to my brother-in-law. He's an expert in all things PC-related and was a contributor to lots of PC magazines at the time.

In five minutes, he gave enough detail for me to draw a sketch of my typical reader. I pinned this picture by the side of my monitor and wrote for this slightly geeky, but very knowledgeable character. It may be a coincidence, but we achieved excellent response rates from the mailshot.

I still work in the same way—with a mental image of today's typical reader.

Even if a client doesn't supply a written brief, I can gain huge insights into their target customers just by thinking about them and using my imagination. You can too. Let's try a simple exercise.

Exercise:
What are people like?

Think of as many words as you can that describe people and write them on the dotted lines opposite. It doesn't have to be the people you're selling to, just people in general. Give yourself two minutes.

To start you off, here are three:

Busy   / Tired   /Ambitious

.........................../.............................../...................
.........................../.............................../...................
.........................../.............................../...................
.........................../.............................../...................
.........................../.............................../...................

We can cluster these personal attributes into two broad groups: those that primarily reflect things the person is running away from and those that reflect things they are running towards. For my three words it goes like this:

Attribute	Away from ...	Towards
Busy		More time
Tired	Stress/overwork	
Ambitious		Money, power

In fact, there is usually a flipside: for every "more" there's a "less" and vice versa.

Attribute	Away from ...	Towards
Busy	To do list	More time
Tired	Stress/overwork	Sleep
Ambitious	Low status	Money, power

The more attributes you can identify for your reader, with their associated feelings of "away from" and "towards", the closer you are to understanding them as a person.

Building a psychological picture of your reader really helps to get a feel for them and what you will need to say to get them doing, thinking, or feeling what you want them to. Of course, you will have all sorts of other information about them (you will, won't you?) and this can help you focus. But knowing their purchasing history is not as important as knowing what kind of a person they are.

Exercise:
How to make an imaginary friend
Here's a simple, five-step plan for getting inside your reader's head—without even leaving your desk.

1   Sit back and relax.
2   Close your eyes.
3   Call them to mind.
4   Imagine them talking to you. What do they look like? How do they sound?
5   Ask them about themselves.

In other words, use your imagination. It's how the world's greatest (and worst) novelists do it. You'll find more vibrant, closely described and realistic characters in *Middlemarch, American Psycho* or *To Kill a Mockingbird* than in many advertising briefs.

Not real people? Sure, I'll give you that. But then, the designated recipients of much business and copywriting aren't either, to judge from the dreary, spiritless tat foisted on them by too-busy-to-think corporate copywriters.

Copywriter's toolkit: Fear and greed
A quick route into your reader's head is to focus on fear and greed. These two emotions are hugely powerful motivators in copywriting. What are they frightened of, and what are they greedy for? Nail these and you've nailed your reader.

The multiple reader problem

We can split all business writing in two: writing for a single reader and writing for multiple readers. (The number of instances when you will genuinely only have only one reader is very small. Even our supposedly private emails tend to get seen by others, as the bewildered, soon-to-be-disciplined authors of what the papers love to call "sex emails" are discovering every day.)

As this book deals mainly with writing for multiple readers, let's look at a common question.

"How can I picture my reader when I have 5,000?" (Or five hundred thousand, or a million?)

OK, it's harder. But you can still do it. Think about your TYPICAL reader. This is the person who embodies the traits SHARED by your diverse readership. If you were writing copy for, oh, I don't know, a major online auction site, then you'd know your reader liked a deal. You'd also know they liked or were tolerant of a certain degree of risk; that they liked excitement. If they didn't, they'd be using mail order or big department stores.

You MUST identify this single reader. To do otherwise is to start down a road to boring, bland and unengaging copywriting, which, whilst sunny and flower-fringed at one end, becomes cracked, weed-ridden and impassable at the other.

It is also to stand a very good chance of contracting a nasty copywriter's ailment called Reader Multiple Personality Disorder by Proxy (RMPDP).

Copywriting case notes: Reader Multiple Personality Disorder by Proxy (RMPDP)

In perhaps one of the strangest cases I have ever worked on, Rebecca T had come to believe, not that she had multiple personalities, but that her readers did. Rebecca's letters would start well enough but then her unfortunate condition would assert itself and she would start to write to all her readers at the same time.

Perhaps you have received a letter written by an RMPDP sufferer. The copywriter uses phrases such as "some of you", "many of you" and "there are those of you." They will often switch from a personal to an impersonal tone of voice midletter. My reaction is to look over my shoulder to see who these "some of" me are.

RMPDP sufferers start seeing all of their readers in front of them at the same time, as if they were gathered together in a concert hall or sports arena. Perhaps because they are aware that certain lists or database segments know something about their products, and others don't, they become unable to focus on an individual reader.

My prescription in these cases is large doses of the second person singular ("you"). I have also found that a drawing or model of a single reader placed opposite the copywriter helps. Most tellingly, I prescribe frequent reminders that readers are alone when they read copy and, except in very rare cases, NOT themselves suffering from Multiple Personality Disorder.

A simple tip is to say "there are those ..." if you need to refer to a wider group of prospects.

Chapter 4
A word about businesspeople

I've spent most of my career writing to businesspeople, usually very senior ones. During that time, I have occasionally met people who say, "Well, obviously, B2B [business-to-business] writing is different because you're writing to a company." But is it? Do we have to write in some sort of corporate-speak because we're writing to people at work? Looking at the letters, emails and brochures I receive, a lot of writers seem to think we do. I don't.

Can a company buy something? Can a company agree to a meeting? Can a company sign a contract? No. No. No. In every business transaction, whether it involves money or not, the parties are always people. Individual human beings. Just because they're wearing a suit doesn't mean they've metamorphosed into corporate drones.

This is an important point. Chief executives, senior managers, call centre operatives: they're all human beings and they're all prone to the emotions, foibles and idiosyncrasies that makes us what we are.

Mini copywriting seminar
HOW TO WRITE B2B COPY THAT SELLS

Here's a powerful four-stage approach to the business of selling to businesspeople.

First—we're writing to sell to people at work

Whatever else we know about our reader, we know this: they're busy. (Not time-poor, incidentally—I'm a fan of plain English.) That means one thing.

We have to be relevant, not brief. An executive won't read a ten-word email if they don't think it's relevant; therefore, short isn't better.

Second—we're writing to sell to people

There's one inescapable fact that a lot of B2B copywriters forget. Businesspeople are still people. And even if they do make decisions based on the business benefits, they are also considering how their decision will affect them personally. The significance for us as copywriters is that we forget our reader's humanity at our peril. Yes, you have to make the business case for a business purchase, but remember this:

One reason CEOs care about shareholder value is because their bonus is based on increases in shareholder value.

One reason an IT manager cares about network security is because their next pay rise will be based on the number of days lost to virus attacks.

And one reason an HR manager cares about absenteeism reduction is because they want the corner office with the view over the river that goes with the HR director's job.

In other words, people make business decisions at least partly for personal reasons. Tap into their emotions, as well as their reason, and you'll get a far more sympathetic hearing.

Third—we're writing to sell

Next, our reader is making a business purchase. As copywriters, we have to uncover and promote the benefits to the business of taking the desired action. Business benefits can be encapsulated in phrases such as:

Save money
Save time
Gain peace of mind (Very useful if you're selling to health and safety managers who don't want to end up in court.)
Make bigger profits
Reduce staff turnover
Improve productivity

You are also usually selling to a decision-making group. So you have to address the needs, motivations and reservations of each member of the group.

Fourth—we're writing

There is no separate language called B2Bish, though to judge from the rubbish I have to wade through regularly, many writers believe the opposite. Use plain English. Why say "prior to" when "before" is available? Why say "substantial revenue stream enhancement" when you just mean "a big hike in sales"?

And it pays to distinguish between technical vocabulary and the threadbare clichés that fly around most organizations. I have many favourites, but high on my list just now is "going forward" (as opposed, presumably, to "going backward"—always useful in business).

Chapter 5
The B-word (and why it's so much better than the F-word)

If you're going to be a great copywriter (and as you've bought this book you clearly want to be) you need to be able to translate the age-old techniques of face-to-face selling onto the page (or screen if you're writing online campaigns). The single biggest issue you need to confront is getting used to using the B-Word rather than the F-word.

Definitions:
B-word = "benefits"
F-word = "features"

People just starting out as copywriters (and even some who are quite a long way down the road) tend to focus on features not benefits. And that's bad news. Why?

Because the reader isn't interested in features. Oh sure, they'll tell you they are; nobody is going to make a purchase without checking out all the features, right?

But it's the benefits that make the sale happen.

People involved in making what you're selling are so close to the product, all they see are features. Automotive engineers enter that profession because they love engines, gearboxes, relays, kit. That's what turns them on and it's why modern cars are so stuffed with gizmos. And, surprise surprise, that's what they want to talk about.

It's the same in any business. I've written direct mail promotions for conference companies for around ten years. And the instinct of the client is often to cut the benefits copy in the brochure to squeeze in as much as possible about the agenda. Conference producers think it's the agenda that interests punters most. But they're wrong. People want to know WHY they should buy, not WHAT they're buying.

You want proof? OK. How about this:

A man—Jim—wants to be sexually attractive to women. If you sell him your hand-stitched leather brogues on the basis that they'll work that magic, he'll buy the shoes. If you sell him aftershave on the same basis, ditto. Sports cars? Toned abs? Hair transplants? Meet the need and you make the sale.

To return to the point at the beginning of this section, copy that talks too much about features is written for the company/manufacturer/producer not the customer/prospect/reader.

Summary

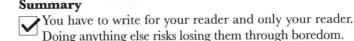You have to write for your reader and only your reader. Doing anything else risks losing them through boredom.

You have to try harder than any other kind of writer because your reader generally hasn't asked you to write to them (and even if they have, they aren't very committed to reading your copy).

Remember that your reader is a human being with all that entails: hopes, fears, desires, vices.

Do your research. Go and find out what your reader is like. Or use your imagination.

B2B copywriting is still copywriting. And you're still selling to people. Forget this at your peril.

Benefits make the sale. Features allow your reader to rationalize their decision to buy.

What do you mean you don't have a plan?

"If you fail to plan, you plan to fail."

Anon

Chapter 6
Yes, but what are you trying to say?

Something happens to people when they have to write sales copy—be it a proposal, a letter, a brochure or a website. They get so wrapped up in the process of writing that they forget to articulate their message clearly—to themselves or their reader.

The copy is long. The copy is wordy. The copy is BORING.

When I've coached copywriters, we often end up looking at a sample of their work, sitting side by side at a laptop. And I always ask the same question: "What are you trying to say?"—because it's rarely clear from the text.

When they start speaking, all becomes clear. They have one or two simple messages that they want to get across and I understand them immediately. "So why didn't you write that?" I ask.

If you want to sell something, you have to break through a wall of indifference, apathy, even downright hostility. People, generally, don't want to receive sales communications (despite what surveys of direct mail recipients tell us). Mailshots are an interruption to the day's work, or pleasure.

The first step in surmounting their objections is to plan what you want to say. Without a plan you're going to spend more time achieving less. Remember the focus of Section One? Your reader? Your plan must revolve around them.

When I ask people at a copywriting workshop what single issue affects their writing, a common response is "writer's block". Now, they're not talking about the tortured condition of the writer sitting alone in a garret staring at a blank sheet of paper, or screen. These are business executives. What they mean is, they know they have to write a sales letter, but they can't think how to start or what to say or in what order.

When I ask how many of them make a plan before they put finger to keyboard, the usual answer is none. And that's the problem. Without a plan you have a real hill to climb. It's hard enough trying to write compelling sentences with fresh phrasing without having to think, "Where am I going with this?"

Think first, write later
The best way to start is to sit down, away from your PC, and just THINK—calmly. Doing this will save time later when you come to write.

There are six big questions you need to ask (and answer):

1   What am I trying to achieve? Change minds? Motivate people? Make someone do something? Buy something?

2   Who am I writing to and what do I know about this person? Remember, even if you are writing something that will be read by lots of people, you should plan it (and write it) as if you were only ever going to have one reader.

3. What do I want to say? You need to have all the facts and background information to hand before you start writing. Make sure you concentrate on your reader's needs, not your own.

4   How much space do I have? Ideally, you should not be governed by artificial length limits when writing. You should say everything you need to and then stop. In the real world, of course, it doesn't work like that. It makes sense to find out whether you have a single side of A4, 500 words or a two-screen email before you start writing.

5   How do I want to come across? Friendly and approachable? Authoritative and knowledgeable? Independent and unbiased? This will affect your tone of voice and the words you choose. We'll look at tone of voice in greater detail in Chapter 16.

6   How long do I have? Deadlines are a fact of life. Learn to come inside them and your client (internal or external) will thank you for it. Over-run and you can kiss that "most popular employee/freelance" award goodbye.

Of these, the most important is number one. In this book, we are talking about copywriting, or at the very least, writing with a commercial purpose. That means you want to get someone to do something for you.

Start with paper, not pixels

Nowadays, most people, including me, write on a computer. We spend our days, or a great proportion of them, staring at a screen. Apart from being bad for your eyes—not to mention your posture, neck, back and the tendons in your arms—it's not a great way to plan. You know you're going to have to spend a big chunk of time sitting at your screen to write your copy, so don't double it by writing your plan there too. Also, that little cursor, blinking accusingly at you in the top left corner of the screen, is as likely to induce writer's block in your plan as it is in your copy. So, here's what I recommend you do instead.

1   Get up from your desk and go and sit somewhere else. Get comfortable. Now you're ready.

2   Paper and pencil is a wonderfully freeing combination. Nothing comes out in perfectly formed type; nothing looks so good that it can't be scrubbed out or scribbled over.

3   Make notes based on all the stuff you've been thinking about. Draw little pictures, if that's the way you prefer visualizing information (it is for one very good friend of mine). Connect ideas with dotted lines or arrows. Draw a mind map. Record your thoughts on tape or digital media if it helps.

4 Try to avoid writing complete sentences. They're hard enough to compose when writing "properly" so don't waste your time on them in your plan—you'll end up spending too much time worrying about your syntax when you should be getting what's in your head down on paper. Writing, a right-brain, creative activity, and planning, a left-brain, logical activity, are two completely different mental processes: it pays to keep them separate.

Jot down bullet points

At this point, you really just want to get all your ideas onto paper, so stick with bullet points. You can just have a few key words that will remind you of the main ideas when you come back to them. To help with the next stage, you could try writing separate points on Post-its. Every time you have a new idea, put it on a new note, then stick them all up on the wall. Once you've got all your ideas you can group them together and see what belongs with what.

At this stage, you should start to arrange your thoughts into themes. There will be a few main ideas under which you can group all your subsidiary ideas. For example, if you are writing a proposal, you might have sections (or themes) headed:

- What's in it for the reader?
- Our capabilities
- Our track record
- Costs and timings
- Background to project

This is still supposed to be a fairly loose arrangement of your ideas, so if you find that there are two or more themes with overlapping ideas, you can split them and decide which points belong in which section. This will help you avoid repetition in your final copy.

Finally, your plan

The end product will be a simple written plan, preferably on a single side of A4. It will have started out as a handwritten document (or collection of Post-its) and will have evolved into a typed plan.

- It will have your goal at the top.
- If it's for long copy, it will have a number of sections that follow on from each other logically.
- If it's for short copy, it will have ideas for paragraphs.
- It will tell a story with a beginning, a middle and an end.
- It will include ideas for alternative ways of presenting your main points.

Believe it or not, you are now ready to start writing. And, if you win the lottery and throw it all in to sail round the Bahamas, your less fortunate colleagues can pick up where you left off.

Chapter 7
Setting out your goals

Let's start at the beginning, with your commercial goals. Nothing complicated here. We just need to answer the simple question, "What's the purpose of this copy?" Remember, your sales copy replaces a personal visit or conversation with a client or prospect. So it has to achieve what you'd achieve (or what your best-performing sales executive would).

Here are a few possibilities:

- Make a sale
- Encourage trials of your product
- Get opt-ins for your email list
- Put your business on a pitch list
- Open an account with you
- Spend more money with you
- Transfer to direct debit payments
- Renew a contract
- Fix a meeting
- Visit your premises

Goals should be what drive your writing—not "creativity", whatever that means.

"Creative" doesn't pay the bills
I like David Ogilvy's take on creativity, "When I write an advertisement, I don't want you to tell me that you find it 'creative'. I want you to find it so interesting that you buy the product." Here's why creativity is a problem for us.

Writers—even copywriters—tend to be creative by nature, and many love playing with words. I guess that figures—carpenters like working with wood and I assume blacksmiths like working with iron. But we need to make sure that our playfulness doesn't become a goal in itself.

The first sign that you should dump a piece of copy is when it makes you smile. If you're feeling so pleased with it you show it to a colleague with a "look at this" grin, that's the second. The clincher is if you ask yourself whether it will persuade the reader to buy and you answer, "No". In creative writing circles, there's a choice phrase for this moment in the writer's life. "Murder your darlings."

So, where were we? Oh yes. Goals. The trick with goals is to make them SMART. Lord knows, the world is awash with management speak as it is, and it's certainly not my intention to add to the flood. But this particular acronym has a place, if only because so few copywriters either know about it or bother to figure out how to apply it to their own.

SMART goals

When I run copywriting workshops, I ask delegates to come up with the words behind the initials for SMART. There's a mumble, then a crescendo as people delve into their mental backpacks to drag out this old management-speak chestnut.

It goes like this:
Specific, **M**easurable, **A**chievable, **R**elevant, **T**ime bound

A goal at the top of your plan that said, "raise brand awareness" would definitely NOT be smart. The immediate and obvious response would be, "from where to where?".

A smarter alternative would be, "recruit 125 new customers spending at least £1,500 each between 1 January and 31 March."

Just for the record, here are a few other goals that, while neither SMART nor sensible, make a regular appearance in many copywriters' minds, to judge from their ads, proposals, sales letters etc.

- Make me feel good about myself.
- Make me and my colleagues laugh.
- Show my boss how clever I am.
- Win an award for advertising creativity.
- Justify the money I spent on a stock shot from a photo library.

Chapter 8
A simple but powerful fast-food mnemonic for creating perfect plans

OK. You've stated your commercial goals. You want more sales. Good. You want £150,000 additional sales this financial year. Excellent. You want £150,000 additional sales at a 30 per cent reduction in cost per sale. Fantastic.

How are you going to achieve these things? What do you want your copy to do?

You need to break down your goals into objectives for your writing. Here's a simple but highly effective little mnemonic to get you on the right track. KFC: what do I need my reader to **know** and **feel** after reading my writing? And what do I want them to **commit** to?

Why is this mnemonic so powerful? Let's break it down …

K   This is all about knowledge. And that means facts. Despite my earlier rant against feature-led copywriting, you do need to include the facts about your product. You're giving your reader the information they need to justify their decision to buy from you.

F   This is the killer point. What do you want your reader to feel? It's a hard question to answer, too. When I'm taking a brief from a client, I always ask this. Some struggle. They'll say, "I want them to feel that we offer 2,000 updated company profiles every month." And I say, "That's not a feeling; that's either true or it isn't. What do you want them to FEEL?"

F-statements should be something like this:
"Excited by the prospect of being our customer."
"Worried that if they do nothing, they could
be missing out."
"Reassured that we are a trustworthy company
to do business with."
"Envious of people who are already our customers."
"Desperate to sign up."

What they all share is unprovability. These are emotional responses and hard to verify, validate or measure. Or not by us mere copywriters, anyway. But here's the big point. If you can get your reader to feel any of these things, they are hugely more likely to buy from you.

C   Sales people call it the close. Copywriters call it the call to action. You have to decide what you want your reader to DO. Maybe it's simple. Buy now. Maybe, though, it's a little more complex. Recommend a friend. Or open their diary and block out two days for a conference in San Francisco when they live in North Dakota. But whatever it is, you need to be specific and direct. Don't be vague here. Tell them EXACTLY what you want them to do, when and how.

I'd say probably all copywriters manage to get the K. It's very rare to find a piece of copywriting where the copywriter imparts not a single fact to their reader. Many will get the C. Even the most jaded hack or wet-behind-the-ears beginner knows you need to ask for something. But few, very few, copywriters ever reach out to the reader and try to elicit an emotional response. In other words, get them to F.

This, as I have already suggested, is where all buying decisions get made. And the good news for copywriters? It's more fun, and more challenging, working on the F. You need to tell stories, paint pictures, involve your reader in your sales pitch and bring them along with you.

If you follow your own KFC plan rigorously (and why have one if you're not going to?) you'll realize you've set the bar pretty high. It takes a lot of thought and then even more hard work to write words that will excite your reader (or worry them) but it's not AS hard as many copywriters think. And the results more than justify your investment. Later on in this book, we'll look at some writing techniques for achieving the KFC task.

Chapter 9
Understanding what you're really selling

Most of us, when we sit down to write some sales copy, think about what we're selling. But too often, we focus on what it IS, not on what it DOES. That's only natural. After all, if you work for a photocopier manufacturer you tend to think a lot about photocopiers. If you work for a designer eyewear retailer, you tend to think quite a lot about designer eyewear.

Trouble is, this is not the road to powerful copywriting. It may be the road to descriptive writing but descriptions of products rarely achieve the sale. And you have to be really wary of letting your production people get involved in writing sales copy. They are so in love with the product that they can't see beyond it. Ask a photocopier designer what they're doing and they'll say "designing photocopiers." As a salesperson, you should be thinking that what they're really doing is designing labour-saving devices.

It's the same with the designer glasses. They don't help people see better than ordinary glasses (that's all to do with the lenses). But they do make people *feel* better than ordinary glasses.

Your customer doesn't care about your product. They just care about what it will do for them. Will it save them time? Save them money? Make them look good? Make them look successful? Make them rich? If this sounds familiar, it should. We're back to the B-word again. You know, benefits. Knowing all the facts about your product is an excellent position to be in. But to make the sale you have to DRAMATIZE them in terms of benefits.

Here are three more examples of products that seem to be one thing when viewed from the producer's perspective and are something else (when viewed from the customer's perspective).

Product: Expensive fountain pen
Appears to be: writing implement
Appears to compete with: biros and pencils
Is: status symbol, upscale gift
Actually competes with: designer wallets, luxury watches, jewellery

---

Product: Harley Davidson motorbike
Appears to be: personal transport
Appears to compete with: other motorbikes
Is: symbol of rebellion and freedom, and amulet against fading male potency (or at least when bought by 44-year-old accountants and not hairy people with tattoos)
Actually competes with: sports cars, hair transplants, male plastic surgery

---

Product: Lottery ticket
Appears to be: Gambling slip
Appears to compete with: Bingo, slot machines, betting shops
Is: Cheap escapism
Actually competes with: Magazines, chocolate bars

Exercise:
What you're really selling
Why not try this with your own product or service?

Product:
Appears to be:
Appears to compete with:
Is:
Actually competes with:

Now that you've started to figure out the true nature of what you're selling, you are in a far stronger position when you want to write about it. Instead of simply describing what you're selling, you can describe what it does for your reader.

Show, don't tell

There's an old sales trainer's adage: "sell, don't tell." That's what I've been talking about throughout this section. It means focusing on benefits, not features. But there's a variant on this phrase that works even better for us as copywriters. It's, "show, don't tell."

We want to paint a picture for our reader. Of life with our product, and life without it.

Copywriter's toolkit: Painting pictures
A simple but effective way to show your reader what your product does for them is to use the opening phrase, "Picture the scene …". Copywriters for cruise liners use it all the time and it's incredibly powerful. It lets you get straight into the right kind of descriptive writing—describing the benefits—and it helps you to do it visually.

The "life without your product" picture is darker in tone, necessarily. You're suggesting negative consequences, a bleak future … though all handled with a light touch; you don't want to depress your reader.

Let's play consequences

To help you find routes into your reader's mind, and the messages that will work most strongly for you, you can use this set of questions. Don't be put off by the apparent complexity. You just need to work through them systematically. And although each pair appears to be a mirror image of the other, the different connotations of "will happen" and "won't happen" lead to subtle but important differences in the answers. Sometimes you can even get powerful selling phrases from your answers. Here they are:

1   What WILL happen if the reader DOES do what you want?
2   What WON'T happen if the reader DOES do what you want?
3   What WILL happen if the reader DOESN'T do what you want?
4   What WON'T happen if the reader DOESN'T do what you want?

I find it helps to fill this out as a grid, like this (and let's suppose I want you to subscribe to my newsletter, *Maslen on Marketing*):

Doesn't do it	**Does do it**
Will happen	**Will happen**
• Will have to rely on own ideas.	• Will become a better copywriter.
• Will miss out on a valuable source of ideas.	• Will get free tips on copywriting.
• Will fall behind your colleagues.	• Will have a monthly source of new ideas.
Won't happen	**Won't happen**
• Won't know what your peers have access to.	• Won't make simple mistakes.
• Won't see the latest thinking on copywriting.	• Won't be stuck in a rut.
• Won't have a source of inspiration others do have.	• Won't have to worry how to keep your writing fresh.

Chapter 10
The killer structure for every piece of copy you'll ever write—online or offline

Back in the 1950s, the American copywriters crafting TV ads for soap powder and household goods used a simple little acronym, AIDA. This age-old formula pre-dates TV though, and any salesman or woman in the last hundred or so years would recognize its essential elements, even if they called it something else. It stands for Attention, Interest, Desire, Action.

It states that in order to make the sale you first have to get your prospect's attention, then get them interested in what you have to say, then make them want what you are offering and, finally, induce them to act.

But because we live in increasingly sceptical, even cynical times, it's also a good idea to get your prospect—or reader—to believe you. So we'll amend the formula to AIDCA. Or Attention, Interest, Desire, CONVICTION, Action.

It's such a powerful recipe for good copywriting that it belongs right in the top drawer of your copywriter's toolkit and it works on the web as well as offline. Let's work through this in detail, so you can see how to apply it to your own writing.

A is for Attention

Before you can start a conversation with someone, you have to get their attention. Otherwise you're just wasting your breath. The same goes for copywriting. They can't listen to your sales message until they've tuned in to your signal. So we have to get their attention. But how? The piece of your copy that does this job is the headline. But we need to tease this one apart a little.

If you're writing a sales email, your headline is your subject line. If you're writing a mailshot, you'll usually have a headline at the top of your letter, but you also have the outer envelope itself. This is your first chance (and maybe your last) to gain your reader's attention.

Which headlines work best?

When a big US advertising agency tested headlines for print ads, they ran the same ad with three different headlines. One delivering news, one promising a benefit and one arousing curiosity.

Which do you think out-pulled the others? (The answer's in the following text box.)

The benefits headline performed best.

When I ask delegates on a writing workshop to vote, they usually go for the teaser headline—the one arousing curiosity. I guess the thinking is, people are naturally curious so if you set them a puzzle, they'll want to find out the answer. Here's why that reasoning doesn't stack up in the real world.

If you write a headline like this one:
   Why are freelance copywriters like dried apricots?

Most people's reaction is, "I don't know and I don't care."

You have to remember that for print advertising, your ad will be nestling among editorial, ie all that stuff your reader paid for and wants to read. Why should they stop doing what they want to do—reading about cars or hi-fi, for example—just so they can solve your little puzzle? If people want puzzles, they do Sudoku.

If, on the other hand, you write a headline like this one:
   How this freelance copywriter can help you double your sales

I think they'll want to know more.

In fact, when the agency went further, and tested headlines that combined all three elements, ie headlines that delivered news, promised benefits AND aroused curiosity, they found they were the most powerful of all.

Writing headlines is probably the hardest part of the copywriter's craft. You have to stop the reader turning the page, trashing your email or binning your mailshot. You have to sum up the main benefit of your offering. And you have to entice them to read your body copy. All in a dozen or so words.

But it's worth the effort. Four times as many people read your headline as read your body copy. So that's where you have to invest your time, too.

When to write your headline

There are two schools of thought on when it's best to write your headline. School one says, you write your headline first. The effort you put in and the time you take mean that once you have your headline, writing the body copy follows naturally and fills out the promise of the headline.

The downside is, you might spend all morning staring at a blank screen or pad until, slowly at first, then faster, small drops of blood begin to ooze out of your forehead.

School two says, write your body copy first, so you get into the swing of selling your product. Then, when you've finished, you'll either have written a headline "by accident" as you draft your copy, or you'll have freed your mind enough to come up with a headline using the concepts and ideas you've expressed in your body copy.

The downside is, you may only arrive at a workmanlike headline and you may also run out of time to do sufficient thinking to write a great one.

And I keep talking about "one" headline. In reality, you want to come up with a dozen at least, then choose the best one, maybe refining and combining a couple of your best ideas along the way. This is not easy. It is hard. Infernally so. And it's one of the reasons people like me can make a living writing sales copy and advertising for other people.

There is no right answer. You just have to try both approaches for yourself and find the one you feel most comfortable with. A tip, though: if you go for option two—writing your headline last—ALWAYS write a placeholder line (a simple stand-in until you write a cracker) to sit at the top of your copy. A placeholder could simply say:

Buy the Watkins Wonder Widget today

(To be honest, that's better than 75 per cent of the headlines you'll see—it at least has the virtue of naming the product and asking for the order.)

One further thought on headlines. NEVER end your headline with a full stop. Even if it appears to be a grammatically complete sentence. Why? Well, think about it. What does a full stop say to your reader? That's right: stop reading. Which is the precise opposite of what you want them to do. Leaving out the full stop encourages them, subtly, to read on, in search of the first stop. By then, you hope you've hooked them into your body copy. Of which, more in a moment.

How long?

"How long should my headline be?"

This is one of those questions that comes up a lot and has no easy answer. Here are three answers:

"As long as it needs to be to get the job done."

"10 to 14 words."

"No longer than a line."

A famous ad headline for life insurance had the powerful headline,

"Cash if you die, cash if you don't"

Eight words, two of which are the emotive and powerful, "cash" and "die".

Remember, you're not telling the whole story with your headline. Just enough to get your reader's attention and make them eager to know more. In general, the shorter the better. Apart from anything else, your designer can make shorter headlines bigger, relative to the body copy; and that, too, will help catch your reader's eye.

Copywriter's toolkit: The headline QuickStart
If you're stuck for ideas for your headline, try starting with "how" or "now".

- **How this sales manager hits his target a full two weeks early, every quarter**
- **How you can save money on your grocery bill without sacrificing quality**
- **How to survive the urban jungle**

- **Now, the new way to cook perfect omelettes ... every time**
- **Now, even better quality, even lower prices**
- **Now, get your golf handicap down where it ought to be**

Pictures pull in punters
Of course, the simplest way to grab someone's attention is to show them an arresting image. That's what newspapers do

all the time. Trouble is, what do you do if you're selling ball bearings? Or management reports? Or bricks? Well, here are three types of picture you shouldn't use:

- A half-naked woman with your product (unless you sell lingerie).
- "Businesspeople" smiling at each other.
- Zebras, sharks, meerkats, dalmatians or any other animal.

Instead, find a way to illustrate your copy that uses or at least relates to your product in context. If it looks dull to you, maybe it doesn't look dull to the reader. You can always hire a professional photographer to light it properly and shoot it from an interesting angle.

I is for Interest

OK, you've got your reader to stop turning the page, hitting the delete button or wadding up your letter and slam-dunking it into the bin. What next? This is when you have to interest your reader in what you're selling. But as we already know, your reader isn't interested in what you're selling. They're interested in what it will do for them. Remember our Radio station, WIIFM? This is the time to start transmitting loud and clear.

Your reader has a problem. They may be feeling stressed, bored, lonely, dissatisfied, hungry, ambitious. Your job is to find a way to tie your product to their problem—as the solution.

One approach is to show them you understand how they're feeling. It's a metaphorical arm round the shoulder. Then you can promise to take the problem away. All they have to do in return is buy your product. Just make sure you're writing about the solution and not the problem. Gets a bit negative otherwise.

Try to answer this question: "How will my reader's life be improved if they do what I want them to do?" Answer it in your first sentence or paragraph. Don't keep them waiting. And as you're not absolutely sure what your reader's true interests are, bring in as many benefits as you can think of. Use concrete, specific examples wherever possible.

Make sure your sales copy is FAB

In Chapter 5, we looked at the difference between benefits and features. But, there's an intermediate stage, where you're talking about advantages. Remember to use the formula FAB—Features > Advantages > Benefits.

The feature is the fact, the information about your product. The advantage is the reason that makes it superior. The benefit is the difference that advantage makes to your reader's life. Here's an example:

F This car comes with bi-xenon headlamps.
A They shine 30 per cent further than conventional halogen headlamps.
B That means you're safer on the road at night.

What is a benefit?

A benefit is anything your reader perceives as valuable or worthwhile. A benefit is anything that your product or service does to make your reader's life easier. Here's a list of benefits:

- Make money
- Save money
- Make your money go further
- Save time
- Get a Hollywood smile
- Enjoy life more
- Be healthy
- Provide for your family
- Keep your family safe
- Help your children learn
- Make friends
- Gain respect
- Get promoted
- Cut down on waste
- Stay on the right side of the law
- Be happy
- Get your dream home
- Get your dream holiday
- Gain peace of mind
- Lose pounds
- Get the perfect figure
- Sleep peacefully every night
- Stop worrying about debt

I could go on, if you like. Now, tell me, what single question do you NOT want your reader to ask if you promise them one of these benefits? That's right: "so what?"

Copywriter's toolkit: The "so what?" test
Read out a line of your copy that you think is selling benefits. Now imagine your reader's response. If they're saying, "so what?", it's not a benefit. When they'd feel stupid asking "so what?", you're home.

Exercise:
Features v benefits

A great little exercise is to take an everyday object (much more interesting than starting with your own product—unless your product IS an everyday object), write a list of its features in a column on the left of a sheet of paper and translate them into benefits in a corresponding column on the right. Be creative.

Like this:

Object: Paperclip	
Features	**Benefits**
Weighs less than a gram	No need to pay extra postage when you use it to keep letters together
Made of steel wire	Won't break and lose your important documents
Recyclable	Helps preserve natural resources
Smooth finish	Won't tear or scratch your papers
Available in a choice of colours	Makes filing easier and retrieval quicker
Galvanized finish	Won't corrode and stain your papers
Packaged 200 to a box	Never run out just when you need one
Made locally	Quality craftsmanship means peace of mind; you're supporting your country's economy

Elliptical shape	Holds your documents more securely so you won't lose them
Can unbend to a straight wire	Use to unstick locked CD drive drawers

Selling NIB: noble, immediate and basic benefits

When you're thinking about benefits, you can really turbocharge your sales pitch by considering them as three discrete types. They're all important and they all work in slightly different ways.

N Noble

These are the benefits that people will admit to being swayed by. Suppose you're selling to chief executives and you have a product that enables them to leave a legacy after they retire.

The noble benefit here is "passing on your wisdom and experience to the next generation of leaders". This kind of thing goes gangbusters with those chief executives who love to present themselves as selfless, disinterested creatures concerned for the welfare of others.

I Immediate

These are the simple little benefits that every product ought to deliver, and we'd be a fool or lazy to leave out. Things such as free delivery, five for the price of four. (Yes, I know the latter could be seen as an incentive rather than a benefit.)

B Basic

As we saw in Chapter 2, you have to know what really motivates the people you're selling to. In the case of chief executives, this is unlikely to be altruism. What kind of people have the drive, ambition and sheer bloody-mindedness to get to the very top? People possessed of towering egos.

Sell them the benefit of ego-massage—say to them "we make you look good"—and you're probably on the right track.

Be specific

When you're selling benefits, it helps to be specific. No, let's be more definite about that: it helps A LOT. People nowadays are (maybe always have been) sceptical about the claims made by sales executives. Rightly so. "Yeah, right, you'll save me money: everybody says that so why should I believe you?"

They'll believe you because you are going to be specific. In other words, you'll tell them how much money they'll save. Your headline could be:

> *How the Watkins Wonder Widget saves this office manager $3,250 a month*

Exercise:
Being specific about benefits

Let's take some random benefits like the ones I mentioned earlier. See if you can find a specific version for the ones listed below. I've done the first for you:

Make money

Make an extra $1,000 a month without giving up your job .

Save money

....

Make your money go further

....

Save time

....

Enjoy life more

....

Be healthy

....

Provide for your family

....

Keep your family safe

....

Help your children learn

....

Make friends

....

Find a lover

....

Gain respect

....

Get promoted

....

Reduce waste

....

Stay on the right side of the law

....

Be happy

....

Get your dream home

....

Get your dream holiday

....

Gain peace of mind

....

Lose pounds

....

D is for Desire

Being interested in something is one thing. Wanting it is another. Things people want form a small subset of the things in which they are interested.

So we, as copywriters, have to ensure that whatever it is we're selling gets into the inner circle. Because there's a fascinating characteristic that belongs to all things that people want. And it's this: when someone wants something, they'll convince themselves they really need it. They'll invent reasons and excuses.

Here's an easy way to think of the difference between needs and wants. (I run this exercise on writing workshops and it always goes the same way.)

Imagine a group of ten women. Ask them to put up their hands if they have ever bought a pair of shoes they didn't WANT. Not many hands.

Now ask them to put up their hands if they have ever bought a pair of shoes they didn't NEED. Lots of hands.

You can work it quite easily with a group of men. Just ask them about gadgets.

Exercise:
Needs and wants

We have four products, A, B, C and D. This is how they stack up in terms of needability and wantability.

A low need, low want   ☐
B low want, high need   ☐
C high need, high want   ☐
D high want, low need   ☐

I want you to rank the products from 1 to 4 for ease of selling, writing your answers in the boxes above.

Now, it doesn't matter where your actual product appears on this table; though if you're in the same position as our notional product A, you've got a rough ride ahead. What matters is how you write about it. You have to make people feel as though it's in position C. That is, they need it and they want it.

Here are a couple of strategies for engendering desire.

Bring it to life

As I wrote the first edition of this book, I was waiting for the classic car I bought earlier that year to be restored for me. When I did the deal for the car and its restoration, I set a budget. But now that I lived and breathed this car, the money had become secondary. Because I WANTED it.

I could picture myself driving it round the country roads where I live. I could smell the leather seats and feel the wood dashboard. I could hear the throaty burble of its Buick V8 engine. Oh boy, did I want this car. In my mind it was already mine. As far as I was concerned I already had it and I was living the life that included the car.

If I were writing a brochure for the restoration company doing it for me, this is EXACTLY the line I'd take in the copy. I'd invite the reader to take the lead role in a story all about themselves and their wonderful life with my product.

And if what you're selling is more of a problem-solver than a need-fulfiller, then paint a picture of the ease and peace that will be your reader's once they buy your product. Make them see that the problem will last only as long as they are content to do without your product.

Restrict the supply

Perhaps the simplest way to make your reader want your product is to limit the supply in some way. Or, to be more specific, in one of two ways.

You can limit the supply in time by having a cut-off date after which it won't be available. Walt Disney does this very successfully in its advertising for video films. You can tweak this strategy a little by making the product available all the time but having a special offer price for a limited period only. Or you can restrict the supply in numbers. This kind of thing, for a conference or special event, maybe:

> *But hurry, demand for places is strong and we must limit attendance to just 120 people. We operate a strict first-come-first-served policy on registrations.*

You could also call this the "eBay effect". Whether you've taken part in an eBay auction or not, you can observe the buying frenzy that engulfs people as the auction draws to a close. It's the bargain-hunter in all of us that drives this behaviour: we don't like to think we're missing out.

Although Milton Friedman, the economist, declared that, "there's no such thing as a free lunch," we all believe we can find that no-strings bargain and walk away the victor. Build that knowledge of the human psyche into your copy and you have the inside track to a sale.

Copywriter's toolkit: Desire drivers
Here are some things you can tell people (or show them) to make them want what you're selling:

- **They have been specially selected.**
- **They are among the first to receive this offer.**
- **People they respect have already bought product X.**
- **Only you/your offer can yield the benefits they want.**
- **They could lose out, especially to a competitor, by not acting.**
- **The supply is restricted, eg only ten free samples/offer closes January 15th.**
- **Your offer is better than any other.**
- **How easy you've made it for them to act.**

C is for Conviction

So, you've caught their attention. You've interested them in what you're selling. And you've figured out how to make them want it. You're almost home (and ready to start writing—relax, the next section is stuffed with practical advice on that stage of the sales process). But ... They're not buying. The cheque book is still in the drawer, the credit card is still in the purse, the direct debit mandate is still unsigned. So what's the problem?

You haven't convinced them.

Overcoming the reader's reluctance to buy is one of the toughest challenges we have to face. It's not that they don't want to buy it. It's just that something's stopping them. Sometimes the problem is natural caution; sometimes it's downright suspicion. Either way, we have further work to do. We have to convince them that the risks of buying are smaller than the risks of not buying (in other words, that they could be missing out on something good).

To convince them, you have to tip the balance so that they feel it's safe to buy.

Here are a few things you can try.

Testimonials
If they don't believe you, they might believe your existing customers. So customer testimonials are great motivators. You see them everywhere: catalogues, mailshots, emails, web pages, ads.

Let's start with a quick exercise.

Exercise:
A question of attribution
Here's a sales claim expressed in four different ways. I want you to rank the claims in order of believability.

A
This is, without doubt, the best method of controlling household pests you'll ever buy.

B

"The best method of controlling household pests you'll ever buy." *Satisfied householder, Paris*

C

"This is, without doubt, the best method of controlling household pests you'll ever buy."

D

"I used to spend hours swatting mosquitoes in my apartment. But not any more. Thank you Bug-B-Gone."
Mme. Marie-France DuPont, 37, Paris

Which one did you have at the top? I'm willing to bet it was D. Which is why you MUST attribute your testimonials. Unattributed, or partially attributed, testimonials just don't cut it with our sceptical readers. (Though did you notice how adding speech marks tips the scales a little?)

Come clean at the start
When I suggest to new clients that we use testimonials in their campaigns, some are ready with a whole pile of letters and emails from satisfied customers. Others haven't ever set about collecting them. Others still are a little worried. "But surely they'll know what we're up to?" is a common concern. Of course they'll know. Because you're going to tell them.

So, here's my five-step guide to collecting and using testimonials.

Step One: Select your storytellers
You want people who like you; your friends and admirers. After all, if they're going to say something positive about you or your products, they'd better be on your side. So ask around. Talk to your sales people. Ask them who your best customers are.

Or look at your database. Who's been buying regularly for five years or more? Who's just made a repeat purchase? Who spent the most with you in the last quarter? You get the picture, I'm sure. These are your storytellers.

Step Two: Decide what you want to get back

Clearly, you have a set of messages you want to reinforce. And since your customers are all busy people, why not save them time and effort by drafting the testimonials yourself? Or get someone like me to do it and save yourself the time.

But remember, you want a distinctive tone of voice for the testimonials, one that even jars a little with the rest of the piece. These have to sound like real people.

Step Three: Get approval

Call your storytellers and explain exactly what you're doing. Ask for their help (people like helping their friends). Then pick three testimonials and fax them to your intended storytellers. Offering them a choice like this makes them feel they are in control and not being herded in a particular direction. Also, suggest that they rewrite the testimonial if they would like to.

Ask them to tick one, then sign and return the fax to you. Bingo! You have your testimonial.

Step Four: Keep it natural

If you have the time, a great way to gather natural-sounding testimonials is to phone your storytellers. Get them talking and when they say something you want to quote, tell them that's what you'd like to do. Then transcribe it, email or fax it to them, and get them to OK it.

If your storytellers have provided their own testimonials—or rewritten your suggestions—avoid the temptation to start editing. Their "unprofessional" style, complete with the odd punctuation error, gives the vital quality you want: verisimilitude—the appearance of reality.

Step Five: Make the most of them

Since you've spent so much time getting your testimonials, it's only right that you really play them for all they're worth. Introduce them in a sales letter as the opinions of customers— "not just more enthusiasm from me."

You could block them together or spread them out to punctuate a long piece of copy. And get your designer to treat them as a very important text element. How precisely they treat them will depend on the target reader and the overall tone of the piece. Here are a few suggestions. Use a different typeface or put a tint behind them. Use oversized speech marks. Pull them out from the text and set them in the margins. Anything, really, as long as it draws the eye. This style of typography also says to your reader: "Hey, this is important, but you can read it without breaking the flow of the rest of the copy."

What else convinces?

Think back to the last expensive thing you bought. What persuaded you to buy? What made you feel it was safe to act— that the risks weren't too high? The sales person, or copy, will have mentioned one or more of the following:

- A free sample
- Statistics, eg of reliability or performance
- A free trial
- Press coverage (positive, naturally)
- Third-party endorsements
- A money-back guarantee

Don't feel you have to choose from this list—use them all if you can. If you only have one testimonial, use it. If you have 50, use them all, particularly on the web, where space isn't an issue. You can maximize your reader's feelings of security by adding in as many safety-factors as you can.

A is for Action

Remember my suggestion for a not-bad headline?

Buy the Watkins Wonder Widget today

This is a call to action. It might even do the job on its own if read by a widget-buyer. And it's what you need at the end of your sales copy.

You can sprinkle calls to action all the way through your copy. After all, giving your reader lots of opportunities to stop reading because they want to place an order is a great idea. Old-school sales guys would look for buying signals from their prospect and, when they saw one, they'd stop selling and start closing. The modern-day equivalent for copywriters would be the hyperlink at the head of a sales email. You're letting your reader buy the instant they decide they've heard enough to say, "Yes".

There are a few things you need to watch for in your call to action.

Ambiguity: it pays not to confuse your reader. If you're selling product A and they think you're selling product B, or a support package, or training in its use, that's bad.

Wordiness: this is not the time for a lengthy essay. You've made your pitch, now come to the point.

Vagueness: don't leave them wondering what you're asking them to do.

To put a positive spin on it, your call to action should be:

Short, Simple, Direct and Clear

- Give them different ways to get in touch and place the order: phone, fax, email, online, post.

- Give them an order form that is clear and easy to complete.

- And make it a command. Order now ... Order by
  January 15th ... It doesn't necessarily mean they'll
  obey but you need to push them off the fence one way
  or another. This is not the place to start using feeble
  phrases like:

"If you'd like to place an order ..."

Copywriter's toolkit: Start at the back
To get yourself into selling mode, write your call to
action first. This has the advantage of getting over
your writer's block (though after this amount of
planning you shouldn't have any) and making you
focus on your goal.

Summary

✓ Without a plan, you are going to face an uphill struggle to
write anything, let alone anything persuasive.

✓ It helps to state your commercial goals right at the top of
your plan—what do you want to achieve?

✓ Remember KFC—what do you want your reader to Know,
Feel and Commit?

✓ Figure out the real reasons why people would buy your
product—they aren't always obvious.

✓ Follow AIDCA, for web and print, and save yourself hours
getting the structure right.

What works? And what doesn't?

"It is with words as with sunbeams. The more they are condensed, the deeper they burn."

Robert Southey, English poet, 1774—1843

Chapter 11
What works

You've identified your reader as a single individual. You've thought hard about what motivates them deep down. And you've spent time planning. You know the benefits of your product and you've come up with a structure that gains attention, generates interest, engenders desire, convinces and calls for action. Now for the tricky bit. Writing.

In this section, we'll look at the craft of writing in detail. How to write hard-hitting, punchy sentences. How to choose words that really connect with your reader. How to use tone of voice to create rapport.

But first, let's examine a few basics.

1   Staying focused on the reader

Every word and sentence you write must mean something to your reader. Think of what you're doing as reeling in a fish. Keep the line taut and you can bring it safely to the net. Let the line go slack—through sloppy writing, or just plain boring writing—and off it goes downstream, in search of watery pleasures.

Your opening sentence, whether on a web page, ad or sales letter, is your main chance to hook readers for the journey. Address them directly, start talking about them and their concerns, needs and wants, and you have their undivided attention. Well, maybe not their undivided attention, but enough of it to start making your case.

From that point on, you have to keep your reader front and centre. Imagine that they're sitting opposite you. Talk to them. Try to gauge their reaction to each new sentence. Have you just said something interesting? Or are they staring out of the window, or looking at a newspaper? Here's why I care so much about this point.

In my early days of selling, I flew to Frankfurt for a meeting with a big Japanese electronics company. I was very nervous, so I had rehearsed a long presentation. This was in the days before presentation software, so I had printed and bound copies, which I gave out to the two managers.

And off I went. The German product manager, perhaps sensing my nerves, listened politely as I trudged through page after page. It was all about our products and, worse, our history and development as a research company. But his Japanese superior just got up and went over to the window looking down at the Messe—the huge exhibition complex in the centre of Frankfurt—and starting making phone calls.

Some 45 minutes later (I still sweat at the thought) he put the phone down and came to sit down again. He looked me in the eye and, very loudly, said, "Air conditioning."

"What do you mean?" I asked.

"We want to know all about domestic air conditioning markets in Europe. This will be very big."

He then proceeded to give me a long list of his requirements, including a number of companies that he thought should be interested in forming a research syndicate to pay for the big consultancy project that would be needed.

What I should have done was walk in, shake hands and ask them, "So, what's top of your list of priorities right now?" And they'd have told me. We could have spent the entire meeting talking about them and their needs, rather than me and my company.

Did we get the job? Well, yes. But I'm afraid it was probably nothing to do with my handling of that meeting.

2   Brevity

We all have a tendency, at times, to keep writing when we should stop. Perhaps we feel we are on a roll and don't want to interrupt the creative flow. Maybe we just CAN'T stop.

There is a widespread and mistaken belief that important subjects call for long-windedness. For example, big projects call for big proposals. Yet all too often their authors are forced to resort to padding. My favourite section in proposals (and one I freely admit to having used myself) is the one headed, "background". This is where the hapless copywriter tells the client what their business is. You know the kind of thing:

> *"Watkins Widgets of Wolverhampton is the leading manufacturer of off-the-shelf and bespoke widgets in the West Midlands, Black Country and metropolitan Birmingham."*

Since the text is invariably cut and pasted from the client's own website, you wonder why anyone bothers.

War is a pretty important subject, so it follows that those in charge will need lots of words, yes? Not necessarily. Just look how much power Winston Churchill packed into this 34-word telegram to General Alexander, Commander in Chief in the Middle East, on August 10, 1942:

> *"Your prime and main duty is to take and destroy at the earliest opportunity the German Italian army commanded by Field Marshall Rommel together with all its supplies and establishments in Egypt and Libya."*

Not much ambiguity there.

"Brevity is the sister of talent," said Anton Chekhov. If you have the talent to be a good copywriter, you must pair it with a ruthless desire to cut your copy to the bone. HOWEVER ...

3   Long copy

In the field of direct marketing, which I've specialized in since 1986, tests invariably show that long copy outpulls short copy. That's a fairly bald statement and needs some explaining. To many people, most people in fact, it seems completely wrongheaded. After all, isn't brevity important? Nobody sits down and reads a great big press ad or an eight-page sales letter, do they? Do they?

Er, turns out they do. And more orders come from the long letter than the short version. More enquiries from the long ad than the short one.

Perhaps the most famous example in press advertising is an ad for Merrill Lynch written by a partner, Louis Engel. Engel was the managing editor at *Business Week* until he was hired by Charles Merrill, the firm's founder.

The ad occupied a full page in the *New York Times*. Seven columns. Tiny type. NO PICTURES. In total, 6,540 words.

It drew 10,000 requests for a booklet mentioned towards the end of the ad (which, incidentally, had no coupon or any other recognizable "response device").

What matters isn't how long your copy is but how interesting it is to your reader.

I've worked with clients who have tested copy rigorously: two-page letters against four-pagers, 100-word emails against 2,500-word emails, one-screen web page against ten-screen pages. And in almost every case, the long copy works harder. Will it work for you? I don't know—you'll have to test it for yourself.

If you've followed my advice on planning, you ought to have plenty of things to say that your reader will find interesting. To put it another way, if you had the chance to visit your reader in their home or office, would you rather they gave you five minutes to make your pitch or an hour? Go figure.

4   Storytelling

Human beings are hardwired to listen to stories. Long before we had writing, we had stories. It doesn't mean that you have to open your ad or proposal, "Once upon a time …"—though I helped write a proposal for a major global publisher that did just that. It means that if you find a way to weave stories into your copy, your reader will be helpless to resist.

In a letter you could use an opening such as:

> *Dear Mr Smith,*
> *Like you, George Brown was interested in investing on the stock market. And using a simple investing technique, George made enough money in a year to retire at 35 and buy a yacht—his boyhood dream.*

In a web page you could write about your service like this:

> *How do I work with you? I could give you an essay on the history and development of executive coaching, but instead let me tell you a story.*

> *David was a senior functional IT director. He was very good in this role. Recognizing his potential as a next-generation leader, his CEO promoted him to the board. Once his initial pleasure and quite natural pride at this recognition passed, David was left with a number of niggling doubts. As he told me:*

> *"Suddenly I have a whole new set of responsibilities that are nothing to do with functional IT issues. How do I present myself as a credible and authoritative voice to my new board colleagues? What do I want to achieve? How far can I go in reinventing myself in this new role without losing sight of my core values and beliefs?"*

And of course, any case study is automatically a story. In the examples I've just given we have characters, a predicament and even dialogue. But notice how they are still relevant to the reader. We haven't forgotten point one.

5   Asking questions

When you're talking to someone, it is very easy to keep their attention. You have eye contact, body language, the rise and fall of your voice and, most important of all, dialogue. That is, taking it in turns to ask and answer questions. With the written word, you are denied all of these techniques. But there are a couple of things you can do to simulate conversation.

First, ask questions. If you've never written in this style before, it can sound a little forced, obvious even. But let me assure you: it works. For headlines or opening paragraphs, web pages or posters. Ask someone a question and I guarantee they will think of the answer. Even if your question occurs half-way through a turgid corporate press release (not that you write those) or a long sales letter. It's human nature. You can load the dice still further in your favour by telling them you're about to ask them a question.

Before I give you a couple of examples, let's remind ourselves of the different types of questions we can ask.

Closed questions

These are the questions that have a yes/no answer.

> *Would you like to buy product X? Have you ever wished you owned product Y? Will you come to our seminar on product Z?*

They are good in sales situations for closing, that is, forcing someone off the fence and (we hope) into a decision to buy.

Limited questions

These offer a choice from a small set of answers.

> *Do you want that in blue or green? Would you like to come to the seminar on Tuesday or Wednesday? Which do you prefer, wine or beer?*

You can use them to engage people without making them think too hard.

Open questions

These have no fixed answer.

> *What's your favourite movie? How many times have you looked at the TV and thought "I could do that"? Who would you most like to go on a date with?*

You're ceding control of the conversation to your reader, since they can take their time thinking about the answer, but most people love being asked this type of question.

Using open questions is a good way to make a connection with your reader. It shows a certain respect if you ask their opinion, for example, and distracts them from your true purpose.

You could say, in the opening sentence of a press release, for example:

> *What makes some people "catch of the day" when it comes to the dating game?*

I think even the most hard-bitten journalist would probably read at least the next sentence. (And remember that, as a copywriter, that's all you ever have to make someone do.)

Using closed questions is good if you can be sure you won't get a "no" answer. Pick your questions carefully and you can have two or three "yes" answers before they've even thought about what you're asking them to do. Here's what I mean:

> *Dear Fred,*
> *Would you like to halve your monthly mortgage payments and still keep your current home? Would you like to take twice as many holidays abroad without breaking the bank? Would you like a new car every two years without taking on unwanted finance costs? A pipe dream? Not any more. Let me explain …*

6   Establishing rapport

Point 5 is all about making a connection with your reader, or, as my word processor defines rapport, "an emotional bond or friendly relationship between people based on mutual liking, trust, and a sense that they understand and share each other's concerns".

Find a bridge between you and your reader, establish that emotional bond, have them feel you understand their concerns and they are far more likely to buy from you. But how? OK, apart from asking questions, here are a few things you can do.

Use your research. If you know that your reader is worried about their children's safety, you could use a phrase like:

> *"It can be worrying being a parent nowadays—so many risks to think about, so many temptations for little hands."*

We're looking for an agreeing nod, a smile of recognition. Whether you have your own children or not is beside the point. You're a copywriter, remember. Get into their head and feel what they're feeling.

Or flatter them. Show them how clever/important/rich/ beautiful they are and they'll want to listen to you all day. Like this:

> *"As an above-average people manager, you see better than most the value of clear communication."*

Copywriter's toolkit: Quick rapport-builder
If you want to make your reader feel clever, just use the little three-word phrase, "As you know" to introduce some fact or statement about their job, industry or the world in general. Like this:

"Dear Mrs Green, As you know, it takes more than just sunshine and rain to make a good garden."

And use appropriate language. If you are promoting a men's magazine like *Maxim* or *FHM*, you have licence to use more down to earth, even earthy language, than you would if you were promoting, say, the *Times Literary Supplement* (for which I have written many letters and advertisements) or the *Harvard Law Review*.

What's interesting psychologically here is that the language doesn't depend on the reader's education or social status, but on the relationship they have with the brand or product you're selling. The same 35-year old man might subscribe to both *FHM* and the *Harvard Law Review*, but you'll be in trouble if you write about the latter as, "the most sorted mag for legal lads and chamber chicks".

7   Fresh ideas

It's fair to describe copywriting as a craft rather than art. But you still need ideas. You still have to be creative. [But see Chapter 7 for a warning note about creativity.] If you're going to penetrate the miasma of other people's marketing messages clogging up your reader's brain, you need to have something fresh and stimulating for them.

You need to stretch for that elusive word, phrase or concept that will stick like a burr in your reader's mind. And, more importantly, have them reaching for the phone or the credit card.

But creativity is an elusive beast. The more you strive to find it, the deeper in your unconscious mind it hides. You need to relax, and let creativity come creeping out where you can use it. Here is a list of 20 things I do to stimulate the flow of ideas. Some of them may not be practical for you. Others may simply not work for you. But I hope a few will help you explore and develop your own approach to creativity.

Copywriter's toolkit: Stimulate your creative juices

1   Go for a walk by the river.
2   Take some hard physical exercise.
3   Write down anything that comes into your head.
4   Pick up a fountain pen and paper instead of sitting at your screen.
5   Use the thing you're writing about.
6   Draw the person who's supposed to be buying what you're writing about.
7   Do five minutes of breathing exercises.
8   Look through an art book.
9   Read poetry.
10 Flick through a book of quotations.
11 Read other people's copy.
12 Write a scene between two people, one of whom has already bought the product.
13 Stare out of the window and put your mind into neutral.
14 Ask your friends what would make them buy this thing.
15 Imagine you're making the purchase decision and decide what would sway you.
16 Look in your ideas book—a collection of phrases and words that occur to you at odd times when you're NOT writing copy.
17 Read books by great copywriters.
18 Turn the ringer off on your phone.
19 Go and work somewhere other than your office.
20 Make something really good to eat.

Chapter 12
And what doesn't

1   **Showy writing**

Remember in Section One, we talked about planning? We had a simple fried chicken mnemonic to help plan our copy. KFC: what we want our reader to KNOW, FEEL and COMMIT.

The one thing we don't want our reader to know is what good copywriters we are (although, paradoxically, you have to be a very good copywriter in the first place to avoid this trap). There may be a case for showy writing in fiction or journalism (though I think not) but there is no place for it in copywriting. Think of your writing as a window through which your reader sees the view on the other side of the glass. We want them looking at the view, not the window.

But, sadly, a lot of poor copywriters (and even more good ones) are so in love with the sound of their own voice that they can't resist bludgeoning the hapless reader over the head with the fruits of their talent. For some reason, this happens a lot in print advertising, especially when the image selected is wildlife-related. You know the sort of thing I mean:

> *"At seventy miles an hour, the cheetah is the world's fastest land animal. Converting oxygen to pure speed at 5.8 litres/second, it makes the savannah a racetrack where only the fortunate survive.*
>
> *Wearing bespoke camouflage designed to disguise its blistering attacks and confuse the unwary on whom it preys, the cheetah is truly a super-competitor.*
>
> *And so is the Acme home office shredder. Capable of handling up to ten sheets of A4 simultaneously, this speedy little number is the fastest document security solution available …"*

HELP! How many ads have you seen that start like this? And who thought that was a good way to use up expensive advertising space? And who signed it off?

2 Jargon

Picture the scene. It's Acme Shredder Co's quarterly sales meeting. Julie Jones, Senior Vice President, Forecasting and Sales Systems, stands up and addresses the meeting:

> *"The bottom line is we have a restricted revenue enhancement scenario that's negatively impacting our growth projections. Unless the ROI on our employee incentivization and motivation scheme exceeds the parameters of our stop-loss position for commission-based promotion options we may have to recredentialize our brand equity customerwise."*

Do people really speak like this? Maybe not—but they certainly write like it. You'll see this stuff all the time if you work for a big organization (even little ones aren't immune). Some of the worst culprits are management consultancies, accountancy firms and government departments.

Is the writer trying to communicate meaning? Or are they more concerned with communicating status? Our job, on the other hand, is clear. We want to get a message as clearly as possible from our head into the head of our reader. Jargon won't do it.

We should draw a distinction between jargon and essential technical vocabulary. There is no substitute for "derivative" if you are in the arbitrage business, but if you habitually refer to a spade as a soil excavation facilitator, you have some work to do.

3 Long-windedness

Wind is one of those ailments that afflict copywriters from time to time. And, believe me, it does nothing to improve your chances of making a sale. Yes, long copy will generally outpull short copy. But remember, that's long interesting copy, not long boring copy.

Some copywriters will, if asked (and plied sufficiently with alcohol), admit to having suffered from some of the more, shall we say, glamorous ailments of the job. They will hold court in the Nib and Quill, the Cursor or the Wordsmith's Arms and regale their listeners with tales of struggle, relapse and ultimate cure.

Few, though, will ever own up to wind. (Though this is one of the most common health issues for copywriters, particularly those in the corporate communications arena.)

For a year or so, I worked for a British government department, editing its internal reports for wider consumption. To compound the problem, the reports were written by management consultants. Here is just one example of what, surely, qualifies as wind:

"The necessary requirement for multiple respondents to be interviewed had inevitable negative consequences on the time elapsed for completion."

Can you work out what the writer meant? I thought I could and called him to check. Sure enough, the translation is:

"Because we had to talk to lots of people, the project took longer."

Other examples of wordiness:

Original	**Translation**
To self-select	To choose
In the interim period between the years of	Between
Our office is situated in the city of Manchester	We are in Manchester
Roughly about 2 to 3 years	2 to 3 years
At the present point in time we are offering	We offer

Copywriting case notes: Wind

For Greg C, wind was an ever-present problem, though owing to a related condition, he was unable to detect his own gassy efforts. Greg would regularly churn out sentences like this one:

"It is our intention to contribute on a quarterly basis to the understanding of the need for greater utilization of primary and secondary customer-facing segmentation methodologies and models."

I didn't know what he meant. And his readers, on whose response he depended for his job, didn't either.

The symptoms of wind are visible to the naked eye: long trailing sentences, slab-like paragraphs and bloated documents.

Surgery was the only option. I cut out redundant adjectives, repetitions, clichés, tautologies, abstract nouns, superlatives and waffle. After a few refreshing redrafts, Greg's copy was able to stand on its own two feet.

4   Talking about yourself

Just before I started to write this chapter, a mailing dropped through my letterbox for a company selling upgrades to a speed camera detector.

Sentence one: *"We've now finished development on our exciting new range of camera detectors."*
So what?

Sentence two: *"I'm delighted to write to you with all the details."*
So what?

Sentence three: *"With so many options to choose from I am sure we have a product that's right for you."*
SO WHAT?

Given that these little gizmos (legal gizmos, I hasten to add) can potentially spare you from endorsements on your driving licence, fines, higher insurance premiums and even a driving ban, you'd think the MD of the company could have come up with a strong opening to his letter.

Instead, he fell into the classic trap of telling me about his own feelings. Many senior managers or directors do this when writing sales documents about their companies. What about KFC? What about Radio WIIFM?

Another example. A company I have worked with for many years sends out proposals soliciting sponsorship for conferences. The company has a globally-respected brand and offers potential sponsors exposure to senior international managers.

Selling the sponsorship deals should have been relatively easy. But the company was missing opportunities. A few years ago, I was asked to take a look at a couple of the proposals. And do you know what the first two words were? *"In 1937…"*

Given this was written in 2003, it's unlikely that the reader was even alive in 1937. The opening section of the proposal then proceeded, at great length, to itemize every stage of the company's history and development. From, yes, you've guessed it, small and humble beginnings to its current position of global significance in its industry.

And somewhere around page 7 of a 16-page document, the first shy little benefit peeped out of the undergrowth hoping nobody would notice it.

It's clear what the writer was attempting to do. Remember the C in AIDCA? Providing evidence of our history and record is a good way to add weight to our sales claims and make our reader feel comfortable doing business with us. But it doesn't belong at the start.

I asked the sponsorship manager why she'd written the proposal like this. And her reply?

"That's how we always do it."

I asked her whether she thought it was a good way to do it. Her answer?

"I don't know, I've never really thought about it."

Historical data might help give you credibility, but it has to be kept brief. Very few people outside your company are remotely interested in what it was doing 40 years before they were born. They're not especially interested in your emotional state, hopes for the future or management philosophy either.

5   Boilerplate
When we're in a hurry, which for many of us is all the time, we look for shortcuts. Little time-saving tricks that allow us to tick off another item on our to-do list. Cut and paste is one way of doing it; another is using those stock phrases we call boilerplate.

There are two pieces of copy that fall squarely into the boilerplate bin, one beginning a letter or email and one ending it. They're known as boilerplate because they are not crafted individually as part of a unique written communication. Instead, they are bolted on as a complete piece of text.

The opening line is: "As a valued client …" Have you ever received a letter or email that started like this? I have. Many times. But what is the writer really saying?

We have clients that we don't value.

I value your custom so little that instead of thinking of something original to say to you I used this hackneyed old cliché.

The closing line is: "Please don't hesitate to contact me." Again, the subtext is …

Please don't contact me.

Using boilerplate is another way of showing your reader you don't respect them. The cumulative effect of all your time-saving shortcuts is bland copy that's impersonal and cold. Cutting and pasting is a related activity and has similar dire consequences. It's time for another story from the medical files.

Copywriting case notes: Cutandpastitis
She was bright. She was creative. She was lazy. Catherine F started sales letters well enough, but the lure of the next project was too tempting. Trying to save time by "borrowing" copy from other documents to complete her own, she contracted Cutandpastitis. One of the worst infections I have ever treated, in fact.

Here is an example. It's from a sales letter Catherine wrote promoting a legal newsletter.

Dear Mr Sample,
If you are anything like the thousands of barristers who have come to rely on The Jarndyce Files, you prize timeliness, insight and case law examples highly. And that's why I am writing to you today.

[A good start, and one Catherine should have persevered with. But read on.]

Recent years have witnessed an explosion in class actions. Widely misunderstood yet often pursued by unscrupulous law firms, class actions have three defining features ...

[Here, we see the tell-tale signs of the infection: a lurch in tone, a baffling digression into the reader's profession and, clearly, another writer's style.]

My treatment was in three parts. First, education. I explained to Catherine the dangers of sharing documents. Then we examined her time management and planned enough time in her day to allow her to relax and complete each document herself. Finally, we tested a new-style letter against the infected version and measured the results. She never caught it again.

If you're in a hurry, do something that doesn't take up much time, like making a cup of tea or a phone call. Rush-job writing is never a good idea.

6 Over-excitement

Try a little experiment with me. Close your eyes for a few seconds and think about an exciting thing you've seen, done or experienced.

Back with me? Now, about that thing you were thinking of. Was it the product or service you promote? Didn't think so. But many copywriters must lead very boring lives. How else can we explain their profligate use of "exciting" to describe their products?

So what exactly is wrong with calling your product exciting? Well, nothing … if you're selling trips in a jet fighter or offering recipients of your mailshot the chance to wrestle alligators at half time in the next Superbowl. But let's be honest. Brutally honest. The products and services most of us promote can legitimately be described as many things but exciting isn't one of them.

Don't get me wrong. You may have a product that will revolutionize management accounting, transform the way companies plan their sales territories, enable senior executives to take fewer risks. And that's great. But all you have to do is concentrate on spelling out for them HOW. In detail.

It's the mark of a lazy copywriter to pin "exciting" on the chest of a brave young noun, pat it on the back and send it into battle. I'm sure you've seen writing of this kind: "exciting" pension plans, "exciting" concepts in office furniture, "exciting" approaches to web-based management information. Can you hear buyers of these products turning to a colleague and saying, "Hey Fred, come and take a look at this exciting toner cartridge"?

Using "exciting" and its siblings "important", "amazing", "unique", "revolutionary" and "fantastic" means you're emoting not evoking. Instead of working hard to arouse the required emotions in your reader, you just pour out your own feelings onto the page in the hope that, somehow, they will transfer to your reader. But let's be honest, how many letters/promotional emails have YOU opened that started, "Dear X, I am writing with news of an exciting new development …"?

And let me ask you this. How do they make you feel? I'm guessing one or more of the following: bored, irritated, patronized, annoyed. It's obvious why, as well. The clanging subtext of this type of copywriting is: I am so bored churning out brochures for my company/product that this is all I could be bothered to come up with. No wonder it doesn't work.

If your reader wants to use those words that's fine. In fact it's brilliant. But they'll only do that if you show them what makes your product so special. Which brings us back to that hoary old line about benefits. Yes, it turns out once again that all you really have to do to sell something is explain to your reader what the benefits are. Calling something 'exciting' is not explaining the benefits.

So here's what to do. Every time you catch yourself about to use a word like "exciting", stop and ask yourself WHY you think your product/service deserves this overworked adjective. Then write that down instead. It's always harder writing about benefits than larding your copy with superlatives, but that's what you have to do. In summary, be specific. Be explicit. And remember, nobody likes being told how to feel about something.

7   Humour

Why do so many copywriters think the way to make the sale is to pack their copy with puns, wordplay and "jokes"? I suspect many are influenced by the very specifically British TV advertising style exemplified in the early days by the Smash Martians, Guinness ads and early Cinzano campaign starring (no other word will do) Joan Collins and the late Leonard Rossiter.

There may be a few product categories, and a few media channels, where that style of humour pays the bills. But for the majority of us, writing hard-working copy to sell business-to-business or professional services, or consumer products of higher value than instant mashed potato, humour is a distraction. Yes, your reader might be smiling, laughing even, but they're not reaching for the credit card.

So how come *The Economist* relies so heavily on humour in its advertising? A couple of reasons spring to mind. The first is that the brand is so huge you don't need reams of copy to persuade someone to go into a newsagent and buy a copy.

Possibly the most famous advertisement for
The Economist, this poster has undeniable
humour; but the underlying message is stark.

The second is that beneath the wit, there is always the same, powerful underlying message: "Successful people buy *The Economist.*" Starts sounding like a benefit when you put it like that, doesn't it? In any case, these ads are only part of a broad communications strategy that also includes direct mail, loose inserts, TV advertising and web-based promotions.

Perhaps picking up on the (apparently) effortless advertising style of *The Economist*, many in-house copywriters (and quite a few external copywriters who should know better) spend their days crafting hopeless sales letters and ads stuffed with lame gags that even a clown would reject.

And, as Claude Hopkins, one of the true advertising greats and a man earning $185,000 a year as a copywriter in 1907 said, "People don't buy from clowns."

8   Subjectivity
Even very experienced businesspeople come over a bit giddy when confronted with a new piece of copywriting. All the more so if you've gone to the trouble of producing a proof for an ad, web page or letter. Whereas they would judge an investment

plan on its likely ability to generate cash, or a new office on its suitability for the number of employees, computers, lathes or whatever, they judge copywriting as a layperson would.

The reaction you'll often hear isn't, "will it work?", but "I don't like it." Or, to be fair, "I like it." The latter is gratifying to the copywriter but it still misses the point. You need to shout, "Who cares whether you LIKE it?"

A simple example. A few companies have tested different typefaces against each other for mailshots to determine whether some generate more sales than others. Courier—the typewriter face you see here—consistently outpulls more "modern" typefaces like Times or Arial.

Yes, that's right. Letters set in Courier make more CASH for the companies that use them than letters set in Arial. But do we hear marketing managers clamouring to use Courier? Do we have corporate communications departments (aka the brand police) issuing edicts prohibiting the use of any other typeface?

It may be hard, but you have to get the people who approve your sales copy to do so based on its likely efficacy, not on their personal prejudices.

Summary

✔ **What works**	✘ **What doesn't**
1 Staying focused on the reader	**1** Showy writing
2 Brevity	**2** Jargon
3 Long, interesting copy	**3** Long-windedness
4 Storytelling	**4** Talking about yourself
5 Asking questions	**5** Boilerplate
6 Establishing rapport	**6** Over-excitement
7 Fresh ideas	**7** Humour
	8 Subjectivity

Section Four

OK, start writing

"If language is not correct, then what is said is not what is meant; if what is said is not what is meant, then what ought to be done remains undone."

Confucius, Chinese philosopher, 551—479 BCE

Chapter 13
The black arts (and a few magic words)

Way back in Chapter 1, we looked at a simple truth. Your readers are more interested in themselves than they are in you. And to keep them reading, you need to focus on them and their motivations. Big surprise, huh? Now we're going to look at five simple techniques you can use to encourage them to keep reading, even when they might not want to. Oh, and by the way, after these five, I have some magic words that will transform the power of your copywriting.

Number one: Broken lists

Everyone likes reading lists. And it's a natural human expectation that if you promise a list of, say, three things, you'll deliver three things. But to keep them reading, why not artificially break the list across two paragraphs? Like this:

> *As a subscriber to* Maslen on Marketing, *you gain three things. First, hot tips on the best way to sell using the written word.*

> *Second, membership of a worldwide community of marketers who value the craft of copywriting. And third, digests of the best new ideas from around the world.*

I defy you not to read the second paragraph to find out how the story ends.

Number two: Teasers at paragraph ends

In fact, we could build on technique number one by encouraging them to read on to the next paragraph. Here's a simple way of doing it:

Second, membership of a worldwide community of marketers who value the craft of copywriting. And third, digests of the best new ideas from around the world. But that's not all ...

There are plenty of other teasers like this. You could say...

And here's why ...
And there's another reason why subscribing makes such good sense.
So why subscribe?
If you're not already convinced, how about this?

Number three: Pages ending mid-sentence

This is another great device that plays on the human need for completion. If you have a letter that goes over the page, make sure the first page ends mid-sentence. Something like this:

Subscribe to Maslen on Marketing *and you are five times more likely to*

You can add a PTO if you like, but my bet is your reader just won't be able to help themselves. They HAVE to turn over. (And do explain to any well-meaning copy-editor that you spent A LONG TIME fixing that final sentence and that they shouldn't "neaten it up" by reuniting it with its tail end.)

Number four: Promises of goodies later on

Particularly appropriate for longer copy, especially online, this technique draws your reader in by weaving multiple lines into your text. There's the narrative they're reading right now, and there's the narrative they'll be reading in a moment. And you can use "in a moment" to achieve the effect. Like this:

In a moment, I am going to reveal to you the five most important errors most copywriters make on the order form. But first ...

Again, you are enticing your reader and involving them in your narrative. They want to know what's coming next and they'll read on to find out.

Number five: The humble PTO

A simple but incredibly effective tool to keep people reading is the PTO (as in "please turn over"). Placed at the bottom of a two-page letter, or a brochure, or a catalogue, it draws the eye and gives them a strong call to action. But …

Don't say PTO, or even "please turn over". You can do better than that. Here are a few things that are far, far more powerful:

> *Details of your special bonus discount, overleaf …*
> *See over for more testimonials …*
> *What do our customers say? See over …*
> *How you could benefit, overleaf …*
> *Details of your free book follow …*
> *Hear what your fellow engineers have to say …*
> *Next, Mrs Smith's story …*
> *Three more reasons to buy …*

As usual, the limit is your own imagination and creativity.

If you know a little about the way people read, you'll be able to draw them through your copy using specific techniques that play on simple psychological truths. Practise the five here to ensure you can incorporate them smoothly into your copy. Now for those magic words.

The six magic words that unlock success

Let's look at a few words that could help you cast your spell.

1   Easy

In the early 1980s I read psychology at the University of Durham. Here's something I learned (apart from the best way to drink Tequila). Ready? People are inherently lazy.

If you can promise to make things happen for them while they sit back with a beer and a good book, they'll thank you for it. So show them that buying from you is effortless. Show them that your product or service is easy to use. Here are a few examples:

Five easy ways to order …
Three easy steps to better copywriting …
The next bit is easy …

2   Quick

Hey, guess what. People are as impatient as they are lazy. Who wants to wait for something they've decided to buy? Nobody, that's who. You know the old marketing adage, "sell the lawn, not the grass seed". Well, tell them that they'll have a lush, deep-pile sward in just seven-to-ten days. Or:

The Sunfish response booster is quick to install.
The results are so quick you won't believe your eyes.

3   Free

One of the original magic words, yet still immensely powerful. If used correctly. In the wrong hands it can kill a promotion stone dead. There are still some copywriters who don't believe in the power of "free". So they try to improve it by adding "absolutely". Er, hello?

Presumably, these are the same people who are completely surrounded by absolutely free gifts that are blue in colour. Better to say how much your gift is worth. That gives it concrete value in the reader's mind. Now, the caveat.

If you're writing an email campaign, you need to be careful. Use Free by all means, but test it. In fact, pre-test it so you know the likely impact on the spam rating of your copy.

4   Now

Various properties this one. As a lead-in to a headline, it suggests the reader is on to something new. As a tag on a call to action, it imparts a sense of urgency. In body copy, it can flip a problem into a solution. Like this:

> *Dear Reader,*
> *Time was, you couldn't buy solar-powered pencils for love nor money.*
> *Now you can.*

5 Please

Amazingly, some of the most powerful magic words are the kitchen-table language we learned as children. "Please" is a good example. You could say:

> *Please read on for more news of this quick and easy route to better writing.*
> *Please click here for details of your subscription options.*
> *Please call me if you would like to know more.*

It baffles me why otherwise perfectly polite individuals forget the pulling power of "please" when writing copy. But hey, they probably don't say "thank you" either.

6 Guarantee

People, generally, crave certainty. When they decide to buy something, one of their greatest fears is that it won't do what the salesman promised it would. How can we allay their fears? How about offering a guarantee?

Now, guarantees are quite slippery little customers. After all, can you really guarantee that your product will perform exactly as specified 100 per cent of the time with 100 per cent of your customers? Of course you can't.

But what you can do is guarantee that it will OR they get their money back. It sounds a lot more positive than it really is. All you're saying is, "My product might not work for you. If that happens you get a refund." What they hear is, "My product will work for you."

Chapter 14
Why your sales copy should be like a bowl of Rice Krispies

There's an elusive quality to all great copywriting, from ads to ezines. On writing workshops, delegates often say they want their writing to be more "punchy". Even though it can be hard to explain in detail, we all know what they mean. Another word would be "snappy". So, given my fondness for food metaphors, let's look at five ways you can give your writing some snap, crackle and pop.

Use power words for emotional kick

Power words connect directly to your reader's brain. You don't have to explain them. You don't have to define them. No need for a dictionary to understand them or a thesaurus to find them in the first place. What's interesting about power words is how a lot of copywriters find it very difficult to come up with them at all.

Off the top of my head, here's a list of 17 power words:

Love	**Chop**
Hate	**Fizz**
Sex	**Crash**
Cash	**Best**
Risk	**Worst**
Care	**Win**
Child	**Lose**
Give	**Burn**
Huge	

Notice anything? See any long words? I see a list of monosyllables, many of which sound great. Most copywriters tend to overlook the sound of their writing, I guess because they're concentrating so hard on what it means. But the best power words do two things—they send a concept and they spark another sense into action in your reader's brain. In other words, you are engaging them more deeply in what you're saying.

When we're writing, we are often concentrating just on getting our message across. Our first draft (and remember that from now on all new copy you write is only a first draft) is full of words that, while they convey our meaning well enough, lack spark.

As you redraft, look for all those floppy, flabby, worn-out words you've used and try to replace them with zingier alternatives. Here are a few phrases in common use and power-words we could use instead:

Weak	Powerful
Cost-effective	Cheap
Impact negatively	Hurt
Optimal	Best
Risk-adjusted	Safe
Upgrade	Boost
Impactful	Striking
Convenient	Easy-to-use
Reliable	Rock-solid
Solve	Crack

Using power words helps your writing stand out from the torrent of garbage spewed out by corporate marketing departments every day. Now, you may feel that some of the examples above aren't quite right for your business or your particular reader. That's fine: you are the best judge of the tone of voice you should use when addressing your customers, suppliers and partners. Just keep on looking for that non-obvious way of expressing your ideas.

Use personal words to sound human

In Chapter 13, we looked at a few magic words that can bring a new dimension to your writing. Here's another one: "you".

"You" is a fascinating word. We use it all the time in conversation (which the best copywriting mimics) but many copywriters shy away from using it on the page (or screen). If you have an academic background, you will almost certainly have been told NOT to address your reader directly in reports and papers.

Many US educational institutions publish guidelines on report writing that specifically command the writer, "Do not address your reader. Never say 'you,' 'your,' or 'yours' in direct conversation to the reader." (We'll pass over that peculiar "to" at the end.) Well, maybe that's OK for academic writing but we're in sales and "you" works.

Back to my undergraduate research into psychology. Do you know what I discovered? The person most people find more fascinating than anyone else? Of course you do—we've already talked about it in this book. You can tap into this narcissistic impulse by using "you" rather than I. Here's an example:

Instead of saying,

> *"Order now and I will send you a free copy of* My Life Behind the Keyboard*",*

say

> *"Order now and you will get a free copy of ..."*

Or:

> *"As a member of the* Copywriting Inner Circle, *you will find your skills as a copywriter exceeded only by your ability to charm your friends, impress your enemies and ensure you always get your preferred seat whenever you fly on business."*

If you do have to write about yourself, "I"—or, at a pinch, "we"—is far better than using your company name. It keeps it personal and involving. Does this work for ads as well as letters, web pages as well as emails? Of course. We ALL want to be talked to as individuals, ALL the time, especially when we're reading copywriting.

Copywriter's toolkit: The 3:1 ratio
As a rule (if you want one), aim for a ratio of three uses of "you" to every use of "I".

Use verbs not nouns

Remember your English teacher at school? What did he or she tell you about verbs? They're "doing" words. And in copywriting, just like in fiction, action is important. Verb-driven writing is active and vigorous. Verbs propel your story. (They're often power words, too.)

But there's a tendency in some copywriters, particularly management consultants (why ARE they so bad at writing?), to turn their verbs into nouns. And there's a name for this affliction: "nounitis". Here are a couple of examples:

nouns
Our *specialization* is the *provision* of IT *solutions*. [Eight words, 44 characters.]
verbs
We *specialize* in *solving* IT problems. [Six words, 31 characters.]

nouns
We focus on performance *measurement*, *management* and *standardization*. [Eight words, 60 characters.]
verbs
We *measure*, *manage* and *standardize* performance. [Six words, 41 characters.]

Copywriting case notes: Nounitis
Ah yes, nounitis. I shall never forget the first time I encountered a case. The patient was a young and beautiful Californian webmaster, Frances F. We

surfed, we drank margaritas, we ... er ... anyway, the symptoms.

Frances was an able web writer who had avoided much of the wide-eyed wonderment that can infect the digital community as they advise the rest of us that, "You can make people want to read on by using a headline."

But Frances had a problem. Her verbs—once so energetic—were gradually disappearing. She experienced a slow spread of nouns in their place; decreased vigour; and a preponderance of words ending in -ment, -ance, -tion and -sion.

Nounitis is often caused by a desire to be seen as important or of high status. The direct cause is excess hot air in the paragraph.

For people like Frances, I recommend surgical removal of noun endings to restore smothered verbs.

 Exercise:
Restoring verbs
Here's a list of nouns. Write in the verbs they stem from:

1	Performance	....
2	Evaluation	....
3	Execution	....
4	Enhancement	....
5	Evasion	....
6	Pronouncement	....
7	Reliance	....
8	Assistance	....
9	Intention	....
10	Production	....

Use Anglo-Saxon words

When people want to sound clever, or "grown-up", they often turn away from the ordinary words they grew up with. This tendency to distrust Anglo-Saxon words results in a leaning towards Latin- or Greek-derived words in their place. This is a shame, because the latter, apart from being harder for most people to understand, are invariably LONGER. Which is a bad thing.

In copywriting, where we strive to connect with our reader, Anglo-Saxon is the best place to start. (And no, I'm not talking about "bad language", just more of those everyday words that we all use and understand.)

Here's a list of 21 random Latinate words and their Anglo-Saxon translations:

Prior to	Before
Post	After
Permit	Let
Disseminate	Spread
Identify	Spot
Terminate	Kill
Residence	House
Aggravate	Worsen
Illuminate	Light
Procrastinate	Delay
Grandiose	Showy
Fortify	Strengthen
Innumerable	Lots
Determine	Find out
Investigate	Look at
Prevent	Stop
Construct	Make
Illustrate	Show
Implement	Carry out
Obtain	Get
Calculate	Work out

Just like our verbs and power words, Anglo-Saxon words tend to be shorter, which is a GOOD thing. But does this only apply when we are writing general consumer promotions or ads? Not at all. It's a common error to assume that if we're writing to businesspeople, especially senior businesspeople, we have to use some kind of high falutin' language where nobody gets a big pay rise but instead receives a substantially-enhanced remuneration package.

Yes, of course, there are issues of register, ie the formality and tone of your writing, when you are addressing different audiences. But these differences are less than many suppose—and what counts is the medium itself: copywriting is, or should be, conversational and unstarchy. You should only reach for the long word if the shorter equivalent won't do.

If anything, CEOs, to whom I write a lot, are busier than average and pay less attention to copywriting than average. So using up their limited attention with long words that need translating is never a good idea.

Be positive, not negative

When they read your sales copy, your prospects find it easier to understand positive language than negative language. Using positives also makes your copywriting sound more, well, positive. Like you want things to happen.

Here are a few negative phrases and their positive equivalents:

Negative	**Positive**
Don't delay	Hurry
Your money back if you're not satisfied	Satisfaction guaranteed or your money back
Don't forget	Remember
There's never been a better time to	Now is the ideal time to

Chapter 15
Good English style for copywriting

In his essay "Politics and the English Language", George Orwell offered the following "six elementary rules" for writers:

1 Never use a metaphor, simile or other figure of speech which you are used to seeing in print.
2 Never use a long word when a short one will do.
3 If it is possible to cut out a word, always cut it out.
4 Never use the passive voice when you can use the active.
5 Never use a foreign phrase, a scientific word, or a jargon word if you can think of an everyday English equivalent.
6 Break any of these rules sooner than say anything outright barbarous.

Orwell was concerned primarily with formal academic, literary or political writing, but his rules form a solid foundation for copywriting, too. Let's take them one at a time.

Never use a metaphor, simile or other figure of speech which you are used to seeing in print

In other words, avoid clichés. If you are used to seeing a particular metaphor in print, then so is your reader. And that means it has lost its visual power and is just a worn-out piece of language. I'm fond of looking for subtexts, as you know, and the subtext of any cliché is, "I am too lazy to think of an original idea so I used this hackneyed phrase because it was easy for me."

Just so we're clear, metaphors and similes are words that stand in for other words, usually with a strong visual feeling. Metaphors replace the word altogether, as in "Our sales director is a bear when we miss our targets." Similes are comparisons: "Our sales director acts like a bear when we miss our targets."

Used well, both metaphors and similes can create strong pictures and ideas in your reader's mind and allow you to emphasize certain points in an original and interesting way. That word "original" though, is the key. It takes a lot of hard work to come up with an arresting metaphor or eye-catching simile. But work is what you have to do if you want to engage your reader and compel them to act as you want to, simply by writing to them. What you must avoid at all costs is worn-out language: words and phrases so tattered by overuse that they impress nobody.

Second-hand similes

Reaching for the well-used simile brings nothing to your writing but the faint odour of second-hand clothes. You may trust a favoured supplier implicitly, but when you write of them that they are as "honest as the day is long" you are doing them a disservice. Why? Because this particular over-worked simile has attained the status of cliché. And like all clichés, it tends to be read as a turn of phrase rather than the literal truth.

Mixed metaphors

> *There's a cold wind blowing through the industry and it's going to swamp us if we're not ready.*

> *The new investment will ensure our competitive edge is our golden goose.*

These are both examples of mixed metaphors, where the writer starts off with one visual idea then concludes with another. Winds can't swamp things (though tidal waves can) and edges can't be geese, golden or otherwise. It's a common fault, but one you should avoid.

Avoid clichés (like the plague)

Clichés infect everybody's writing; they are part of how we speak. But although you want to write as you speak for tone, you don't for style. Clichés come in three basic varieties:

General, everyday clichés
One hand washes the other
Nose to the grindstone
Leave no stone unturned
Diff'rent strokes for
diff'rent folks
Without a shadow of a doubt

Business clichés
Get our ducks in a row
Blue-sky thinking
Win/win situation
Pushing the envelope
Low-hanging fruit
Best practice
Going forward
Ballpark
Global
Strategic

In-house
This space is left blank for
you to fill in your own special
favourites.

....
....
....
....
....
....
....
....
....
....
....
....
....

Never use a long word when a short one will do

As children, we learned to write using short, simple words. Then, as our confidence grew and our education progressed, we graduated (sometimes literally) to using longer and more complex words. It all started to go wrong when we began deliberately choosing longer words, even though there were perfectly acceptable shorter words at our disposal.

Most people contract thesaurusitis at some point in their careers; the question is, how strong is their immune system? Can they resist the infection and return to a simpler, plainer way of writing that their readers will understand?

I'm sure you've come across a few infected specimens in your time. This kind of thing:

> *"Our primary objective is the collation and dissemination of best practice."*

When all the writer really means is:

"Our main aim is to find out what works best then share it."

Don't get me wrong; long words aren't bad—no words are. But using a long word when a shorter one would do is a bad habit. The writer is more concerned with showing off, or with pleasing themselves, than with ensuring their readers can understand what's been said.

Exercise
Shorter words
If you can make your meaning clear using a short word, rather than a longer synonym, do it. You will spend less time writing, and your reader less time reading. Write in a shorter equivalent for each of the following:

information	....
facilitate	....
fortunate	....
immediately	....
construct	....
objective	....
anticipate	....
sizeable	....
exceedingly	....

If it is possible to cut out a word, always cut it out

"Omit needless words."

As well as being co-author, with EB White, of *The Elements of Style*—one of the best little books on the English language you'll ever buy—William Strunk, Jr coined this pithy phrase that all editors and writers should have tacked onto their foreheads. How do you stick only to what's necessary? Remember these four rules.

1   Never use a descriptive word when a noun or verb will do

Do you remember back in school, the day your English teacher introduced you to adjectives and adverbs? Those lovely words to add information about those boring old nouns and verbs? Suddenly it wasn't just a cat sitting on the mat, it was a fat, furry cat sitting lazily on a circular, silken mat.

That childlike enthusiasm for decorating sentences with descriptive words stays with us into adulthood and our careers. But all too often we forget that the English language offers us such richness of vocabulary that there are huge reserves of under-used nouns and verbs that in themselves do the describing for us. And, in the process, keep our writing tight.

In the example above about our old friend the cat on the mat, one of the five descriptive words is redundant. Have a look and see if you can spot it. A clue: you could replace it, and the word it qualifies, with another. Yes, it's "lazily". In fact, we could say slouching, lounging, sprawling, reclining, loafing, lazing or lolling.

Unless they provide extra information, adjectives and adverbs are just a lazy copywriter's excuse for not thinking harder. Here's how to use more precise words instead:

- Not a huge house but a *mansion*.
- Not a forward-looking executive but a *pioneer*.
- Not a respected company but a *standard-setter*.

It works for adverbs, too:

- Don't work hard, *strive*.
- Don't think creatively, *innovate*.
- Don't perform impressively, *excel*.

2   Avoid meaningless adjectives

There is another way adjectives contribute to waffle: when they are used purely for emphasis. Here are a few examples:

- A serious crisis—compared with a light-hearted one, we assume.
- A loud bang—as opposed to the quiet kind, presumably.
- A terrible war—unlike a quite mild war?
- An important development—as if you'd be talking about unimportant ones.

In the first three, the nouns in question supply all the meaning the copywriter needs: crises, bangs and wars are by their natures serious, loud and terrible. In the fourth, the copywriter is striving for significance without giving the reader a reason to believe them. And this is by far the most common use we see in copywriting.

Managers proud of an achievement naturally want others to think well of them, and imagine (perhaps too fondly) that using words like "important", "essential", "invaluable", "groundbreaking", "unique" and "special" will help. In fact, the reverse is true. Cynical readers (and who isn't cynical when faced with another example from the super-smashing-great school of copywriting?) will naturally assume they are being presented with a humdrum idea being hyped. And, in 99 cases out of 100, they'll be right.

The rule is, use adjectives to add information, not emphasis. So, we might write about:

- An environmental crisis
- A distant bang
- A civil war
- A technical development

3 Make a few redundancies
While working out what to say next, a lot of us need to keep the sentence ticking over. There are lots of handy phrases that help us out but we should strike them from any written communications because they add nothing except breathing space, which should be invisible in writing.

Here are a few of my favourites:

Redundant/wordy phrase	Simpler alternative
At this point in time	Now
The reason for this is because	Because
Due to the fact that	Because
It is important to bear in mind that	Just start with whatever comes next
It should also be noted that	As above
A pair of twins	Twins
Completely surrounded	Surrounded
Orange in colour	Orange
Surrounded on all sides	Surrounded
Close scrutiny	Scrutiny
Close proximity	Near

4   Beware the abstract noun

Perhaps striving to sound more important, many copywriters fall into the trap of attaching adjectives to abstract nouns rather than the concrete nouns they properly qualify. Examples include:

The website has undergone a significant level of updating.

The information was of a confidential nature.

We update the report on a quarterly basis.

Take out the abstract noun and you get:

The website has undergone significant updating.

The information was confidential.

We update the report quarterly.

Never use the passive voice when you can use the active.
Did you know there's a little tune-up you can perform, a tweak
you can give your writing that makes it punchier, sharper, more
personal, more involving AND shorter? All without sacrificing
any of your meaning? Oh, you did? Well you can skip this next
bit. Still with me? Good. I want to talk about the active voice.
Or rather I want to show you the active voice. Look at the next
sentence:

> *The cat sat on the mat.* [Six words.]

This is the active voice. The subject—*The cat*—comes before the
verb—*sat*. Notice how the cat is doing something to the mat, ie
there's some action.

Putting the same sentence, the same action, into the passive
voice gives us this:

> *The mat was sat on by the cat.* [Eight words.]

Now, the subject comes after the verb and the focus is on the
mat. The mat (the object of the verb sat) is just lying around
having something done to it, ie it's passive.

And look what happens to the sentence length. An extra two
words might not seem like a big deal, but that's a 33 per cent
increase in length for no extra meaning. Imagine if your copy
was all in the passive voice—it could be up to a third longer
than it needed to be.

But here's another reason why you should avoid the passive
voice. It is impersonal and imposes a distance between you and
your reader. Here's the start of a letter it's all too easy to imagine
receiving from a company you are complaining to:

> *Dear Mr Smith,*
> *It is regretted that our service was found to be unacceptable.*
> *An investigation has been launched and the results will be considered*

> *as soon as they are received from our complaints department. At that point, a decision will be taken as to how your request for a refund should be dealt with.*

That example is all in the passive voice. See how flat and unemotional it sounds? How unconcerned the copywriter seems to be; how you are being fobbed off? Now, they might be deeply saddened by your letter, but because they are wedded to the passive voice, their concern isn't getting through.

Here's how they might have written it:

> *Dear Mr Smith,*
> *I am sorry you found our service unacceptable. I have launched an investigation and will consider the results as soon as our complaints department gives them to me. At that point, I will decide how to deal with your request for a refund.*

Now we can tell who's doing what and how they feel about it. And just look at that opening sentence. It defuses the situation by apologizing and taking responsibility for the problem.

There are a few ways you can check for the passive voice.

1 Look for the word "by" in your text. It will pick up a lot of perfectly OK uses but also a lot of passive verbs. If you have a word processing program, use Edit>Find in the toolbar at the top of the screen.
2 Look for any form of the verb "to be" plus your main verb. For example, *was* (past tense of "to be") *received* (main verb).
3 Use the grammar checker in your word processing program. The readability statistics will give you a percentage of passive sentences.

You should aim for as low a score as possible—zero is often the ideal. But don't be a slave to this rule, or to any of the other numerical targets I give you in this book. They are only guides. Ultimately, your own judgement as a copywriter must prevail. If you feel that a sentence reads better with a passive verb, then leave it that way. Just be sure that you've tried it both ways.

Here's an example of potential ambiguity caused by too rigid an insistence on the active voice:

Passive
> *The car was chased by the dog belonging to Mr Smith.*

Active
> *The dog belonging to Mr Smith chased the car.*

Look at the final five words of the active voice version. Who exactly is chasing the car? There's a moment of ambiguity before your reader sees the truth and that's one moment too long. A quick rewrite gives you:

> *Mr Smith's dog chased the car.*

Excellent.

Never use a foreign phrase, a scientific word, or a jargon word if you can think of an everyday English equivalent

Those who wish to be thought educated have always used foreign words to make their ideas sound more impressive than they really are. In 17th century restoration comedies, for example, fops would dust their speech with French words like icing sugar on a croissant. Latin and German make regular appearances on the "most pretentious" list, too. But we want clarity—and that means plain English.

Here are just a few no-nos (or should that be non-nons … nein-neins?) to get you going:

Foreign	Plain English
frisson	shudder
trauma	shock
prima facie	at first sight
vis-à-vis	on/to/about
raison d'être	purpose
weltanschauung	world view

Apart from making yourself more readily understood, using plain English has another beneficial effect on your writing. It makes it shorter. Saving your reader time by giving them more succinct copy is always a good thing. Especially online.

Break any of these rules sooner than say anything outright barbarous

This is really our "get out of jail free" card. It means you should focus, above all, on the impact your words have on your reader and the sound your writing makes. Even at the best of times, copywriting is only tolerated, not welcomed. So giving your reader something light and effortless to read is preferable to forcing them to plough through heavy clay, however "correct".

The perfect sentence (and how to write it)

A strong house is made one brick at a time. And strong copy is written one sentence at a time. Learn what makes a good sentence (and what makes a bad one) and your task as a copywriter is a whole lot easier.

There's an art to writing a good sentence, and I want to give you a head start. My one overriding piece of advice? Put it this way: what do copywriters and liberal judges have in common?

They both like short sentences.

Most business writing, whether for letters, proposals, reports or brochures, suffers from the same fault: overlong sentences. And researchers agree that the single biggest block to understanding is long sentences. You know, the kind that start off simply enough, but then develop a life of their own, meandering over multiple topics without ever coming to a satisfying conclusion, forcing you to perform increasingly tough feats of memory as you struggle (or perhaps you have given up by now) to retain a vague sense of what the writer had in mind when they began this marathon. [*That's enough long sentences—Ed.*] But what do we mean by a long sentence?

Let's start with an arbitrary figure. You should aim to limit your sentence length to 16 words—ON AVERAGE. Try to write only 16-word sentences and two things will happen. First, your brain will explode. Then your reader's will. Life's too short in any case to spend it counting out the words in all of your sentences. And, luckily, you don't have to.

If you are one of the many people who write copy in Microsoft® Office Word, you'll find it gives you a very nice little set of readability statistics for each document. I'll show you how in Chapter 21. The most important is words per sentence (WPS).

Now, if you run this little test on a few pieces of your writing and you're getting 16.3 or 17.1, I'd relax. But if you see numbers starting with 2 or 3 (yikes!), you have some work to do. Go back through your text and you'll probably find the culprit or culprits. It doesn't take many to throw your average out: fix these and watch as your WPS magically settles down in the mid-teens.

The fact that we're talking about averages is important for another reason (apart from stopping your brain exploding, I mean). Say your WPS score is 16 dead. That means there are a few eight-word sentences and a few 24-word sentences.

The short ones are easy meat for your reader's brain, allowing them to decode your meaning instantly and without effort. Perfect. That means they have more energy and enthusiasm when you, occasionally, ask them to work just a little harder.

If you can come inside this target, which as I said at the beginning is somewhat arbitrary, so much the better. Write copy with a WPS score of 12 or less and you can more or less guarantee that your reader will be able to understand exactly what you mean. And that, let's remember, is the essence of effective writing.

Copywriter's toolkit: The hot spot
When you are writing to influence someone, pay attention to the final word in your sentence. This is the prime spot, the word that lingers in the memory. So keep it for powerful words. Here's an example, first of how not to do it, then a better version:

Your customers will be delighted when you use our product.

Use our product and your customers will be delighted.

Chapter 16
Tone of voice: What is it and what to do with it

Tone of voice is something we normally don't think about too hard. You're cross: you speak in a cross tone of voice. You're happy: you speak in a happy tone. You don't consciously set out to talk like that, it's just the way you are. Your emotions are naturally expressed through your voice as well as your face and your body language.

But turn to the written word and there's no sound. So why do copywriters, in particular, talk about tone of voice? Well, it turns out there are one or two techniques you can use to simulate different tones. Getting it right is critical because, in the absence of face-to-face or even telephone contact, your words are all you have to establish a relationship.

In general, you should write as you speak, a subject we've touched on a number of times already in this book. At the risk of repeating myself, choose plain, simple language. Write down what you'd say if someone asked you about your product or company in the pub. (Remember, this chapter is only about tone of voice, not style. You can always edit your copy later on to give it a little more formality.) Aim for conversational, natural language that would sound OK if you were saying it out loud.

Copywriter's toolkit: Read it out loud
The easiest way to judge the tone of your copywriting is to read it aloud. Would you be happy reading your text to a customer down the phone, or to their face? If "yes", good—you have a great tone of voice for selling. If "no", bad news. Why are you embarrassed by what you've written? Must try harder.

One method of varying tone of voice, and the emotional freight your words carry, is to use what linguists call moods. These are just ways of putting a sentence together. Here are five moods and their emotional connotations:

Mood	Use	Feeling
Indicative	Statements of fact	Neutral
Interrogative	Questions	Open/interested
Conditional	Bargaining	Looking for a win/win
Imperative	Instructing/ordering	Bossy/authoritative
Subjunctive	Hypothesis	Exploring possibilities

Suppose you were writing to someone about a seminar you were holding. Here are five ways of approaching the subject:

Indicative	We are holding the seminar next Tuesday.
Interrogative	Are you coming to our seminar next Tuesday?
Conditional	If you come to our seminar next Tuesday you will receive a free pen.
Imperative	Attend our seminar next Tuesday.
Subjunctive	If I were to offer you a discount, would you attend our seminar?

There is no right or wrong mood to choose, but you can see how each produces a subtly different feeling and will lead to a different emotional response from the reader. Picking the right mood for the right purpose is your job as a copywriter.

You can also use contractions, eg "you'll" instead of "you will", "I've" instead of "I have".

Many people, warned off contractions at school for so-called formal writing, never regain confidence. But for most kinds of copywriting, judicious use of contractions will help you simulate that all-important conversational tone. They should be invisible to your reader in any case.

There's a lot of crossover between tone of voice and plain English. Much of this book focuses on techniques that, when you use them together, almost force you into a natural, warm, human tone of voice.

Copywriter's toolkit: You're not in court
There's one particular style of writing that a lot of people affect, I assume, in the hope that it makes them sound important. To my ear, they just sound pompous, like a 19th century lawyer. Ready?

Hence, we can see that ...
Thus, it's clear that ...
Indeed, we can safely say that ...

Do they ever use these words in speech? I think not. Of course, if you want to sound like a barrister from the reign of Queen Victoria ...

Chapter 17
Why punctuation is a sales tool

Although this book is not a textbook, I want to take some time to cover a subject you probably last thought about at school. I know you use punctuation all the time, but how often do you spend time weighing up the benefits to your copywriting of, say, a comma versus a semi-colon? Or a colon versus a full stop?

If you're anything like the people I coach and train in copywriting, you've probably answered "never". Or "hardly ever". And that's OK. We're all so busy trying to hit deadlines, get the ad written, move on to the next task on our "to do" list, that fiddling about with punctuation is the last thing on our minds. But …

Get punctuation right, understand how to use it effectively, and you can give a boost to your copywriting that will make people a) read and b) buy. And as you become more proficient as a copywriter, your own taste and style will start to play a greater part, shaping the way you use certain punctuation marks for particular effects or tones of voice.

Remember, punctuation helps your reader make sense of what you've written. Understand it, in other words. And if they understand it, they can act on it. And that means sales.

My intention is not to provide a thorough guide to the rules for correct punctuation (if such a thing exists). We'll leave that to the academics. What I do want to do is give you a few pointers on the best way to use the main punctuation marks in a copywriting context. Let's start by dispensing with a myth.

Time for a breather?
Ask any group of people what punctuation is for and most of them will tell you it's to let you take a breath. Wrong. The main

purpose of punctuation is to clarify your meaning. (You can also use it to create subtle rhetorical effects, such as irony; but let's be honest, if you're writing a sales email and you're using irony, something, somewhere has gone wrong.)

It's true that when you're reading very long sentences out loud, taking a breath is advisable unless you want to collapse, blue-faced and gasping, on the floor. But for most of us, most of the time, written communication is for reading internally. People just breathe when they need to, regardless of whether you've inserted a comma, a semi-colon or anything else.

Don't be tempted to put a comma where you would pause for breath; for example, before an important word at the end of a sentence. Here's an example of what I mean:

Our company is driven by one word and that word is, passion.

The comma is unnecessary (and just plain wrong). It's a style of punctuation that reflects the oral roots of all language and it was popular until the 18th century, at which point the importance of oratory began to wane and writers increasingly came to see punctuation as a syntactical rather than rhetorical tool. The aim was to replicate the pauses that a speaker would use to dramatize what they were saying.

Why is punctuation a sales tool? Because if you can make your meaning clear—or clearer—then your reader will understand you better. If they understand you better, they are more likely to do what you want them to. So let's run through the major punctuation marks and how we can use them to greater effect.

Comma

A simple sentence needs no commas. Like that one. But start introducing extra information for your reader to chew on and you need commas to help you separate the extra bits from the main idea. These extra bits can come at the beginning, the middle or the end. If they come at the beginning or the end, you need to mark them off with one comma. If they come in the middle, you need two. Here are three examples based on a straightforward no-comma sentence:

[straightforward idea]
The report covers customer service.

[extra bit at the beginning]
Published on Friday, the report covers customer service.

[extra bit at the end]
The report covers customer service, something we take very seriously.

[extra bit in the middle]
The report, written by our managing director, covers customer service.

The big thing to remember here is that you MUST use a pair of commas when the extra bit comes in the middle. Fail to do this and you risk ambiguity. In the last example above, omitting the second comma results in a (brief) feeling that the MD covers customer service, rather than the report.

You also use commas to separate items in a list. Most people tend not to use a comma after the penultimate item; the "and" does the trick of separating it from the final item. Like this:

Our corporate values are honesty, service, quality and passion.

Semi-colon
Some of the world's greatest and most successful writers have had trouble with the semi-colon. It's quite possible to avoid it altogether in your writing: a full stop will always do. But you are depriving yourself of a valuable tool if you ignore it. Here are the basics.

Joining sentences that belong together

Some sentences are so closely related that separating them with a full stop drives a wedge between two linked ideas. When the second sentence amplifies, illustrates, comments on or expands the idea conveyed in the first, you can use a semi-colon to indicate the connection. Like this:

> *The trade visit to China was our first; we plan a further three over the next year.*

> *Our company was founded three years ago; we have already doubled our turnover and profits.*

Notice how, in each example, we could use a full stop instead of a semi-colon. The advantage of doing so would be shorter sentences. But following that rule slavishly would result in writing that was less elegant and less clear to the reader.

Separating groups of words that contain commas

You may need, or want, to write a long sentence. As a result, you may end up with lots of clauses (those "extra bits" we talked about earlier) separated by, and containing, commas. However good you are as a copywriter, you're putting your reader through a lot of work to decode your syntax and your meaning.

Using semi-colons is a simple and effective way to restore a little order and give your reader strong pointers as to where new ideas start and finish. Here's what I mean:

> *At Watkins Widgets, we believe in delivering a quality service, irrespective of the size of the account, producing the best widgets we are capable of, using the latest technologies and manufacturing techniques, and meeting every deadline we are set, whether that means hiring extra staff or working through the night.*
> [A pile-up of clauses.]

> *At Watkins Widgets, we believe in delivering a quality service,*
> *irrespective of the size of the account; producing the best widgets we*
> *are capable of, using the latest technologies and manufacturing*
> *techniques; and meeting every deadline we are set, whether that means*
> *hiring extra staff or working through the night.*
> [Order restored.]

You should also use semi-colons when a list contains
items that are either long groups of words, or groups of
words containing commas. Here's an example:

> *There were three people on the sales course: Judy, a new recruit,*
> *David, who had recently been promoted by John and Sally, the head*
> *of marketing.*

See the ambiguities without semi-colons? Who's the new
recruit, Judy or David? Had David been promoted by John
or by John and Sally? Let's put things in order:

> *There were three people on the course: Judy, a new recruit; David, who*
> *had recently been promoted by John; and Sally, the head*
> *of marketing.*

Colon

The colon is a more serviceable mark than its half-sister, easier
to understand and easier to use correctly. In copywriting, your
main occasion to use a colon is when you want to introduce
a list, as in the following example:

> The Online Marketing Insider *helps you in three ways: it gives*
> *you new ideas, it saves you time and it keeps you in touch with the*
> *latest trends in digital marketing.*

You can inject a little tension into a sentence by putting the list
items before the thing they describe, making your reader sit up
and take notice. Here's what I mean:

Lightweight, strong and 33 per cent more flexible than its predecessor: three reasons why the Sunfish tongue depressor belongs in every GP's bag.

More generally, you should use a colon when the first half of a sentence promises something that you intend to deliver in the second half. Or when you create a feeling of curiosity with a statement that you intend to resolve. Like this:

Being a good copywriter is about more than using punctuation correctly: it's about selecting and using every word wisely and well.

Notice how in the above example, the part that comes after the colon is a sentence in its own right. But it needs the first part for the reader to make sense of it.

In doing this, you are often using a colon, like a semi-colon, to join two related sentences together. Opinions vary on when to do so, but you can think of the colon as introducing an emphatic point, especially a contrast, rather than simply a following-on thought.

Our research shows one thing above all others: people like people.

Always remember this about housewives: they're our customers.

Our competitors might not believe their customers are important: we do.

One word of caution. Never put a colon after the word including. The following example is wrong:

We offer a variety of marketing services including: copywriting, design and strategy.

The including signals to the reader that what follows is a partial list. A colon, on the other hand, indicates that what follows is the entire list.

Full stop

At last, my favourite punctuation mark. Why? It's simple really: full stops bring sentences to an end. And unending sentences are probably the single biggest obstacle to reader comprehension. In fact, let's be more definite about that: long sentences ARE the biggest obstacle to reader comprehension.

It's true. Every single academic research study on comprehension and sentence length finds that the former decreases as the latter increases. And given that the full stop is the punctuation mark you use to end a sentence, it follows that it has to be the most important.

Bear in mind that ambiguity is a killer in sales. Or in any other field where you are writing for influence. If people don't understand what you're saying, how on earth are you going to persuade them to do what you want them to? Let's have a quick look at our new best friend.

It sounds simple doesn't it? Use a full stop at the end of a sentence. But where is the end of a sentence? A lot of people have trouble deciding. This fault is most usually demonstrated in the form of the so-called comma splice, where a sentence runs on to another, joined by a comma instead of being separated by a full stop. Look at these examples:

> *Our customer service department now has five staff, we will recruit two more in the next month.*

> *Customers are important to us, without them we have no business.*

> *Our plan is for 50 per cent sales growth over the next two years, after that we will consolidate and concentrate on profitability.*

In each case, the comma has been wrongly used: a full stop is required. Cast your mind back to school and your third-year

English teacher, Miss Syntax. She told you that a sentence contains a subject, a verb and an object.

In the first example above, *our customer service department* is the subject, *has* is the verb and *five staff* is the object of the first sentence. *We* is the subject, *recruit* is the verb and *two more* is the object of what should be the second sentence. When you introduce a new subject, you are starting a new sentence. That means you need a full stop before you go any further.

My best advice on full stops is to use them early, and often. Early, because that means you have written a short sentence. Often, because that means your average sentence length is less.

Unless you have compelling reasons for doing so, avoid semi-colons and colons in favour of full stops. Your writing may lack a little elegance, but the gains in readability and comprehension far outweigh the losses. (Of course, if you can write elegantly and concisely then carry on regardless.)

Question mark

Question marks go at the end of questions. Duh! But make sure what you have is a genuine question. The following two examples will show you what I mean:

John Jones asked what we were doing with our surplus widgets?

"What are we doing with our surplus widgets?" asked John Jones.

The first is incorrect. It is a straight declarative sentence including indirect speech. The second is fine: the question IS a question and is enclosed in inverted commas for good measure.

Inverted commas

Sometimes called speech marks, inverted commas are most commonly used to enclose quotes, ie somebody's direct speech.

Whether you use singles—'blah, blah, blah'—or doubles—"blah, blah, blah"—is a matter of taste, whether personal or corporate. Here are two examples, one right, one wrong, of how to use inverted commas to report speech:

> *Jenny Smith, our CEO, said, "We are on target to achieve 35 per cent growth this year".*

> *Jenny Smith, our CEO, said, "the company was going to be on target to achieve 35 per cent growth this year".*

In the first example, the words enclosed by the inverted commas are the actual words Jenny Smith said. In the second, they are not.

Never use inverted commas to enclose a figure of speech, a metaphor or a piece of jargon. All of the following examples contain needless inverted commas:

> *We will have to "think outside the box" if we want to achieve our targets this year.*

> *It's a case of putting our "nose to the grindstone" and getting the job done.*

> *This copywriting guide is the marketing industry's "bible".*

Why are these wrong? Because, in each case, the function of the enclosed words as metaphor or figure of speech is clear to the reader in the first place. Nobody imagines a group of executives locked in a box, trying to think outside of it. Nobody thinks of workers literally applying their noses to a fast rotating carborundum stone. And nobody thinks a guide to copywriting is the Bible. What's happening is that the copywriter is drawing attention, self consciously, to their writing. Saying, in effect, "look at me, I'm using a metaphor." It's the written equivalent of those people who do that double-finger dink in the air when they're speaking metaphorically.

Exclamation mark

Please don't imagine that using an exclamation mark is going to make someone excited about what you're saying. If you've said something dull, or expressed an interesting idea badly, tacking an exclamation mark onto the end won't repair the damage. In fact, you are sending several negative signals to your reader:

"Look at me, look at me, I've said something cool."

"I am at the same level as Internet spammers."

"I am an unoriginal copywriter who fondly imagines you will be impressed by exclamation marks."

It's the linguistic equivalent of canned laughter, or, as F Scott Fitzgerald had it, the sound of the writer applauding himself.

Apostrophe

Apostrophes cause more trouble than any other piece of punctuation. But the rules are clearer than for almost every other mark.

Rule 1: Use an apostrophe to indicate missing letters (contractions).

Like this:

Order now and you'll receive a free MP3 player worth £19.99.
[You will.]
I've enclosed your gift vouchers.
[I have.]
You haven't responded to my invitation to our champagne reception.
[Have not.]

Used subtly, contractions can impart a conversational tone of voice to your writing. Yes, they are frowned on in academic circles, but we're business people not professors of English.

Rule 2: Use an apostrophe to indicate possession

This is where people go astray. But it's simple. To form the possessive, use 's regardless of the final consonant, unless it's a plural ending in s.

So it's:
> *Fred's ball*
> *Charles's ball*
> *The children's ball*

But:
> *The monkeys' ball*
> *The boys' ball*

There are a few exceptions (aren't there always?) to the rule.

Possessive pronouns don't take an apostrophe ...

> *His*
> *Hers*
> *Its (Not to be confused with it's meaning it is.)*
> *Ours*
> *Yours*
> *Theirs*

... and ancient and religious names omit the final s even though they are singular.

> *Jesus' teachings*
> *Moses' law*
> *Isis' temple*

You DON'T use apostrophes to indicate plurals; despite what your local greengrocer might think, the word is tomatoes, not tomatoe's. And it's CDs not CD's, FAQs not FAQ's and RFPs not RFP's.

Ellipsis points

Ellipsis points are those three dots you see in the middle of sentence ... or, occasionally, at the end, like this ...

They properly indicate missing words, although you can also use them less formally to give the sense of a mid-sentence pause or a cliffhanger ending to a sentence. Here are three examples:

For omitted words in a quote for a corporate press release:

> *"We're all really happy with the new website ... a vast improvement on the original," said Fiona Smith, chair of MegaCorp's customer user group.*

The original quote, in full, might have said, "We're all really happy with the new website. After a lot of false starts we now have a vast improvement on the original." The PR manager, rightly suspecting that journalists would be more interested in the false starts than the vast improvement, edited the offending phrase out, replacing it with ellipsis points.

As a mid-sentence pause:

> *Nine times out of ten you won't need our services ... but isn't it reassuring to know that we're here for that one time when you do?*

As a cliff-hanger ending at the end of a paragraph in a sales letter:

> *You also benefit from our patented non-slip technology that means fewer accidents at your factory. But that's not all ...*

A note: the correct number of dots is three and only three. Two just looks as if you hit the full stop key twice by accident. Four or more makes you look dopey.

Chapter 18
Stuff you learned at school you can forget

Remember those "rules" we were all taught at school that now drag along behind us, hobbling us just at the point when we might say something pithy? Here are three you might recall:

"Never start a sentence with 'and'."

"You mustn't end a sentence with a preposition."

"You mustn't split an infinitive."

Never mind whether you remember what prepositions and infinitives are (we'll cover that in a minute). The point is, they simply aren't rules at all. Yes, your teacher told you they were. Mine did, too. But generations of teachers have been suckered into the same game. Why?

It's all the fault of a few crusty old classics scholars in the 19th century. They decided that English—a healthy mongrel of a language—ought to conform to the breeders' rules for Latin and Greek, pedigree languages both. Their pronouncements have passed down, unchallenged by most, and are now held as sacred truths. But there is hope.

Open your copy of *Fowler's Modern English Usage*, or *Usage and Abusage* and you'll see these rules described, variously, as "prejudice", "superstition", and leading to "artificiality and awkwardness."

But remember, keeping your reader in front of you at all times means paying attention to their feelings about the language. If they are the sort of person who recoils in horror from a split infinitive, then you'd better not include any.

Split infinitives

The infinitive form of most verbs looks like this:

To sit
To write
To decide
To go

You split the infinitive when you insert an adverb between "to" and the verb it precedes. Like this:

*To **lazily** sit*
*To **quickly** write*
*To **immediately** decide*

And, in the most famous (and intergalactic) case of all:

*To **boldly** go*

In Latin, the infinitive form of the verb is a single word, so it would be impossible to split it with an adverb. Hence your rule. But English is not Latin.

Stylistically, you should be aiming for a combination of clarity and elegance. If you can say what you have to say without splitting an infinitive, then that's the better route to take. But if it feels and sounds more natural to use a split infinitive then use one and use it boldly. Look at this example:

The client failed fully to consider our proposals.

Here, the copywriter is so afraid of the split infinitive, "to fully consider", that they have unwittingly created ambiguity. Was the client's failure complete or was their consideration of the proposals incomplete? Look how much clearer the sentence is with a split infinitive:

> *The client failed to fully consider our proposals.*

It's worth pointing out that most people have a hazy notion that it's wrong to do this. So unless you can be sure your reader won't notice, or care, it's best to avoid split infinitives when you can.

Ending a sentence with a preposition

Prepositions are those words that describe the relation of one thing to another:

> *The monkey was **in** the cage.*
> *The car pulled up **next to** the kiosk.*
> *The hunter hid **behind** the tree.*

Traditionalists frown on prepositions placed at the end of a sentence. These pedants (or sticklers as they'd like to see themselves) would mark you down for writing:

> *A preposition is something you shouldn't end a sentence with.*

They'd prefer to see

> *A preposition is something with which you shouldn't end a sentence.*

But this is another of those rules whose roots are in Latin. The Latin word for preposition is *praepositio*. It comes from the verb *praeponere* meaning "put before". No less an authority than the *Oxford Dictionary of English Grammar* refers to this "rule" as a "prejudice". Fowler refers to it as a "cherished superstition". Modern authorities agree that the best guide to the correct placing of the preposition is your ear. If it sounds right it is right.

Like all these rules to do with the arrangement of words, they may be helpful, especially since there are always a number of possibilities for arranging the words in any given sentence. But you don't have to be bound by them.

When Winston Churchill was presented with a particularly clumsy piece of writing, tortured into the "correct" form, he replied, "This is the sort of rubbish up with which I will not put." So it's perfectly OK to write:

That's the brick I hit the pedant with.

Starting a sentence with "and" (or "but")

I don't know where this rule came from. But I'm willing to bet you had it drummed into you at school roughly two days after "a is for apple".

I suspect it has something to do with "and" and "but" being conjunctions, ie "joining words". Your teacher's thinking being, therefore, that you can't have "and" at the beginning of a sentence because there's nothing before it to be joined to what comes after it. But "and" also has the sense, "furthermore". And "but" the sense, "however". In other words, they are joining this sentence to the one that came before it.

There's not much to say on the subject except, YOU CAN DO IT. Bolts of lightning will not appear from the heavens and strike you dead. Indeed, the translators of the King James Bible clearly felt it was perfectly acceptable practice. Here's sentence three of Genesis:

And God said, "Let there be light"; and there was light.

Lest the Bible not be your preferred ammo when defending your next business letter from sniping colleagues or managers, how about *The Economist?* Pick up the current issue and I guarantee you'll find sentences (sometimes even paragraphs) beginning with "and" and "but".

Summary

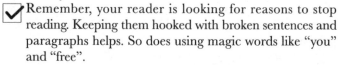 Remember, your reader is looking for reasons to stop reading. Keeping them hooked with broken sentences and paragraphs helps. So does using magic words like "you" and "free".

☑ Inject some snap, crackle and pop into your copywriting with power words, short words, Anglo-Saxon words and good old plain English.

☑ Aim for a natural, warm, conversational tone—it's how you'd speak to your reader face-to-face.

☑ Punctuation is there to make your meaning clear. Getting it right means people are more likely to do what you want.

☑ If you find a sacred cow grazing in your writing, pull out your gun.

Dressed to impress?

"Great designers seldom make great advertising men, because they get overcome with the beauty of the picture—and forget that merchandise must be sold."

James Randolph Adams, American advertising executive, 1898—1956

Chapter 19
Editing your work

At last. You've typed the final word. It's finished. Er, no. What you have in front of you is your first draft. And your first draft is never good enough to send. In fact, if you only have enough time to complete a first draft, I'd suggest you spend it doing something else instead.

Someone once said, "writing is rewriting". What they meant was that to create something good, you have to view writing as a process. Editing—rewriting, if you prefer—is the major part of the process. This is your chance to evaluate what you have written and judge it. Here are ten questions you might ask of your first draft:

1   Does it speak to your reader in language they will understand and respond to?
2   Does it fulfil your stated purpose (remember your plan)?
3   Is it clear?
4   Is it concise?
5   Is it interesting?
6   Is it ambiguous?
7   Is it attractively laid out?
8   Does it contain waffle, unnecessary words or clichés?
9   Does it tackle the issues in the right order?
10 Have you used graphics or pictures to explain or illustrate key points?

How much is the right amount?
One of the most common questions I am asked is, "How much should I write?" If you're working in a marketing department, you might have come across, or even taken part in, the debate about long versus short copy.

The answer is, write as much as you need to, then stop. For your first draft, it's best to overwrite than underwrite. Overwriting is easier. You don't have to edit your work as you go along. You can get all of your thoughts down onto screen/paper without worrying too much about elegance or the precise tone of voice you want to convey. Then, you can edit it, or, to be more brutal, cut it.

Write too little and you may be left scratching around for extra words to boost your copy to the required length. That has two disadvantages: first, you have to keep everything you wrote for your first draft, good or bad; second, adding stuff in afterwards can cause structural problems, breaking the flow of your "complete" copy.

What should you cut?
You should cut everything that doesn't meet your stated purpose for the copy.

If you are writing a sales letter, and the stated purpose is to make your reader place a trial order, anything that makes them do something else, or nothing at all, is bad and has to come out. If you are writing a business report whose stated purpose is to persuade your board to release funds for further work on a project, you must cut anything that makes them think you shouldn't get more money.

How many drafts?
I've already said that one draft isn't enough. So how many is enough? To stand even a halfway decent chance of achieving your goals, you need a minimum of three drafts. But don't worry. That doesn't mean two complete rewrites. Rewriting is going back to your blank sheet of paper and starting afresh. It rather implies you haven't spent enough time planning what you want to say. I'd define redrafting as zero-ing in on your target, using progressively more sensitive tools.

Those three drafts go like this:

One   Initial attempt, warts and all.
Two   Spell-checked.
Three Printed out and proof-read.

But look at how minimalist that editing process is. No rooting out unnecessary sections, let alone pruning unnecessary words. No revising the tone of voice. No attempt to check structure or style. All you can really say is, it leads to a product that doesn't have any mistakes in it.

For a three-quarters decent attempt, I'd aim for five drafts:

One   Initial attempt, warts and all.
Two   Broad assessment against plan.
Three Checks for structure and unnecessary sections, paragraphs, words.
Four   Review for tone of voice, metaphors, fresh expressions, style, punctuation.
Five   Printed out, spell-checked and proof-read.

And you need to be bold. Taking your first draft and tinkering around the edges isn't enough. Here's a table of tools you should use on your drafts, in order:

Draft number	Cutting tool
1	Chainsaw
2	Hedge trimmer
3	Shears
4	Scissors
5	Scalpel

It's worth remembering that the law of diminishing returns applies to copywriting, just as it does to spreading fertilizer on fields (some cynics would say there is more than a passing resemblance between the former and the latter). Each successive draft improves the copy, but by increasingly small amounts.

And there can come a point where new drafts reduce quality, particularly if other people get their mucky paws all over your copy. The following chart illustrates the process.

Redrafting and copy quality

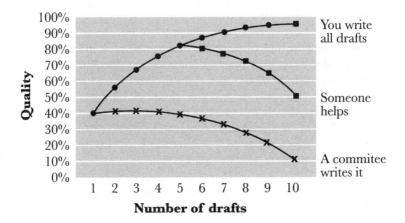

You write all drafts

Someone helps

A commitee writes it

Number of drafts

Chapter 20
Proof-reading

Right, we're nearly there. It's drafted. Redrafted. And edited. Now it's time to check it. And this goes double—triple—if it's an email.

You know, it's always puzzled me how otherwise intelligent people can spend time drafting an email to a client and then hit "send" without even reading it over on screen, let alone on paper. How do I know they do this? Because I have seen actual emails where the client's name is misspelt. Now, what do you think this says to the client? "I care about you"? No. "Your business is important to me"? I don't think so. "I want you to know that I respect you"? Oh, please.

In fact, your not-so-hidden subtext is, "Hey. I'm talking to you but I'm too busy and important to check that I've spelled your name right. I just assume you're going to buy from me anyway". Recently, a client wondered aloud in a meeting whether bad business writing cost her company money. It does. It means lost sales, loss of goodwill, dents and dings in your reputation.

So here's how to ensure those horrible outcomes don't happen to you.

First of all, you have to get into the habit of printing out your copy and checking it on paper. For a start, reading print is easier on the eye and less tiring, so you are better able to concentrate and focus on the job at hand. Also, somehow, it's a slower process (and it needs to be). I've had people look at me as if I were mad for suggesting they print out emails and proof-read them. "But that's so slow," they all shout.

These, though, are often the same souls (soles?) who are happy to email reports to their CEO with spelling mistakes in them. Yes, checking your writing is slow. But then, it's not as time-consuming as trying to repair the bad impression your intemperate or badly written email has made on your reader.

Second, you have to leave a little time between writing and proof-reading, ideally, a day. But if you don't have that much time then at least an hour. If you try to check your work as soon as you've finished writing, your brain will simply correct your errors without telling you. You'll see what you meant to say, rather than what's there in front of you in black and white.

There is a way to short-circuit this time lapse. Get yourself a proof-reading partner. Agree to check each other's work. That way you can hand it over as soon as you're done. Of course, this assumes your partner has nothing to do all day except wait for your plaintive request to, "Check this over for me would you—oh, and by the way, it has to go out by 11.30."

Copywriter's toolkit: Check one thing at a time
When you're checking your writing, it's a good idea to check for one thing at a time. Focus on spelling, for example, first. Then grammar. Then punctuation. Then word choice. Then errant double spaces. This way your brain doesn't get confused by competing demands. Believe me, you'll spot more errors this way.

Another approach is to check levels of text one at a time. So, you could start with main heads, then section heads, quotes, footnotes, flashes, callouts, picture captions, hyperlinks and, finally, body copy.

Spell-check
Nothing marks you out as uneducated or lazy faster than spelling mistakes. You're insulting your reader if you send them copy with a spelling error. The subtext is, "I care so little about you

that I haven't even bothered to check my writing for spelling errors. You do it."

Spell-checking is about more than pressing a button/clicking a mouse. Electronic spell-checks are great tools but they have their limits. They will let through any word that's spelled correctly, even if it's not the one you wanted. Here are just a few of the possible confusions they won't pick up:

Going/gong
In/ion
Can't/cant
We're/were
From/form
Except/accept
The/he/then

A notorious problem with spell-checking is our own feeling of busyness. You know, you've finally managed to crank out your first draft. Now all you really want to do is see the back of it. So you zip through it with spell-check, blithely (blindly?) accepting a "change all" recommendation without looking at what you're being offered. Happy to see "seals" instead of "sales"? You might have to be.

What if I'm not a good speller?
Not everybody is. It doesn't matter. You just have to be a good checker. And here's another tip.

Buy and use a good dictionary. I use the *Shorter Oxford*; colleagues in the US are probably more familiar with *Webster's*. If you're not sure how to spell a word you want to use, look it up. It's a great habit to get into and one that might help increase your vocabulary.

Of course, I could also argue that if you want to use a word so unfamiliar that you don't know how to spell it, maybe you should be searching for a simpler alternative.

Deep down (and quite close to the surface, too) I believe that spelling errors are LESS important than those involving punctuation. Your meaning is usually unaffected by the former but can be reversed by the latter. Having said that, most people find it easier to spot spelling errors and they will usually draw the same conclusion: you're uneducated and/or lazy. Make a habit of checking your work using both software and your eyes.

Copywriter's toolkit: Five steps to error-free copy
If you can't be bothered to proof-read, you're probably in the wrong job. Try telesales: no-one can HEAR how you spell.

If something's worth saying in writing, it's worth checking. Remember: if you don't spot your mistakes, others will. You'll effectively publish your own ignorance and/or sloth.

So here's my bullet-proof, cast-iron, gold standard for proof-reading.

1   Print out your copy.
2   Start at the back and work to the front.
3   Start at the bottom and work to the top.
4   Start at the right and work to the left.
5   Use a white piece of paper to mask off
    the preceding line.

This technique destroys your brain's ability to make sense of a piece of text. You force your brain to consider it one word at a time. By slowing yourself down to the pace you last managed when you were six, you see each word separately and you WILL catch the errors.

Chapter 21
Checking readability

One of the best and easiest checks you can do on your writing is the one for readability. This is about how easy it is for your reader to understand you. So clearly, the more readable your text is, the higher the chance that your reader will do what you want them to.

And it turns out that checking for readability involves absolutely no work on your part whatsoever. Can you click a mouse? Of course you can. Well, you can check for readability. Here's what you do (this assumes you're using Microsoft® Office Word 2007. If you're not, my apologies; there's a similar routine in earlier versions).

In the bottom left of the Word Options Proofing screen, there's a little check-box saying Show readability statistics.

Microsoft product screen shot reprinted with permission from Microsoft Corporation.

Make sure there's a tick in the box. Now, whenever you run a spell-check on your copy (which you do every time, right?) you'll get a little summary of the readability statistics at the end. Here's what it looks like:

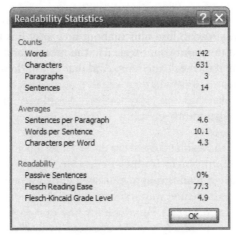

Microsoft product screen shot reprinted with permission from Microsoft Corporation.

These scores relate to the first three paragraphs of this section. The bottom set of figures are the ones that interest us here, although remember how we looked at average sentence length in Chapter 3.

- Passive sentences gives you the percentage of the text using the passive voice. Hooray for me. None.

- Flesch Reading Ease is a formula developed by Dr Rudolph Flesch—a world expert on readability. It's based on sentence length and the number of long words you use. The higher the score, the better. A score of 60 per cent equates to plain English.

- Flesch-Kincaid Grade Level relates to US grade school reading ages. A score of 7.0 means seventh graders could understand this text. That's a reading age of about 12 years.

Now, this doesn't mean your audience is 12 years old. Nor does it mean that your adult audience has a reading age of 12 (though they might). But remember, your reader has very little investment in reading your text. That means they are unlikely to be giving it their full attention. And that means their effective reading age is lower than their actual reading age. So it always pays to make your text easy for busy people to understand without concentrating on it.

If your Flesch Reading Ease score doesn't look too good—under 50, say—the problem is almost certainly down to sentence length. Have a read through your copy and pick out any long sentences. Is there any way you can reduce them, or split them in two, or even three? Also, look for any unnecessarily long words. If you routinely say "intoxicated" instead of "drunk", and "assistance" instead of "help", you have an easy way to boost readability.

Get into the habit of checking readability and it eventually becomes second nature to opt for easier and more readable ways of expressing yourself. In fact, it becomes somewhat addictive.

Chapter 22
Layout—what can you do to help your reader

This chapter isn't exactly about writing; it's about how your words look on the page or screen. But after all the effort you've put into your copy, wouldn't you like to be sure your reader will be able to read it?

We are going to look at some of the simple ways you can lay out your copy for maximum effect. Some of the easy things you can do to help your reader find their way around and read your text without too much eye strain. And some of the horrors that can make their lives impossible.

Signposting

List of contents

If you are writing a report, or a longish brochure (say, eight pages or more), you should consider providing a list of contents. This is the simplest and most effective navigation tool ever invented, yet many copywriters simply ignore it.

Maybe they think their readers want to spend their time guessing the location of the stuff they want to read about. Perhaps they want to force their readers to wade through the whole document. Who knows? But give your readers a list of contents and they can head straight for the bits that interest them. And that's important. You're saving them time.

Remember to include page numbers in your list of contents, not just a numbered list of sections. And then, remember to add page numbers to your pages. If the document is on A4 paper, you might consider using dotted tab leader lines to take the reader's eye from the chapter or section title to the corresponding page number.

Footnotes

Sometimes, you need to explain things—technical words or phrases—or clarify the sources of statistics or comments. You could do this in the run of text, inserting the relevant material in a clause bounded by two commas. But this disrupts the flow of your sentence, and it's only really background information, so it doesn't belong in the main body of your writing.

Instead, use footnotes. You add a reference number in your text like this[1], then add a numbered footnote at the foot of the page containing the relevant information.

Colour-coding

Colour-coding is an excellent way of dividing a long document into manageable chunks. You could combine colour with a list of contents for an instant visual reference system in a catalogue or corporate brochure. You see this technique used widely in mail order catalogues.

Arrows

If you want to point someone somewhere, stick an arrow in front of their nose.

 Like this

Flashes, starbursts and marquees

To highlight important bits of your text, you can put keywords or short phrases into those little graphic elements designers call flashes, starbursts or marquees. Readers tend to go to these first so they are a useful way of communicating your main points quickly.

---

[1] You can set off footnotes under a thin rule for extra clarity and elegance (like this).

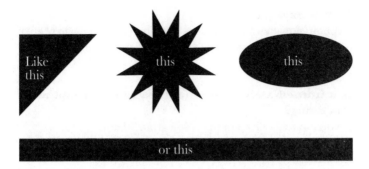

Just make sure your designer uses graphic devices in keeping with your overall style, tone of voice and target reader's expectations.

Graphics
Whether you are designing your document yourself, or employing a designer to do it for you, the question of graphics inevitably comes up. At the lowest level, you have clipart. At the highest, original photography and illustration. Whatever form of graphic you use, and I do think they are a good idea for lightening up the text and adding visual interest, you must ask these questions:

What is its purpose? Is it helping my reader understand the text? Is it moving them closer to my commercial goal?
Often graphics appear to be there purely as decoration. This is not good enough.

Is it a cliché?
Too many ads, brochures and websites use images of clocks and cogwheels, cheetahs and chessmen. Too many feature improbably good-looking executives shaking hands or smiling at their computer screens. You can do better than that.

Does it have a caption?

Captions are attention-grabbers, and are read immediately after looking at the picture itself. They are a great place for a little stealthy selling.

Is it immediately clear what the graphic is and what it is doing?

If you puzzle your reader you will annoy them.

Headings

We looked at headline writing in Chapter Ten. Here I want to focus not on what you say but on how you lay it out. The important thing is to decide on a typographical scheme for your headlines and stick to it. A simple scheme might look like this:

1 Main heading Univers 20 pt bold

2 Section head Univers 16 pt bold

3 *Sub-section head* Univers 12 pt bold italic

Consistent schemes create order and therefore help guide people through the text. Whenever your reader finds another H2, they know they are reading a new section. Whenever they see a new H3, they know they are still within the original section, but now getting new facts.

Point sizes

As a general rule, you should aim for a point size small enough to allow you to fit a reasonable amount of text on to a page and big enough for your reader to be able to see it without a magnifying glass.

Be wary of designers who return proofs to you with your carefully crafted text reduced to a small block of tiny type on an achingly beautiful white background. They don't have to read the stuff, much less act on it.

As a minimum, I would suggest 10 pt Arial and 11 pt Times New Roman, or their visual equivalents if you are using other typefaces.

Typefaces

For the purposes of readability, we can focus on a single attribute of typefaces: serifs. Serifs are the little tails at the ends of letters.

Serifs do two things. They make it easier to read individual letters and they lead the eye horizontally along the line. Both of these functions aid readability (or they do in print, but more of that in a moment).

Here's the same word in a sans serif typeface—ie a typeface without the little tails.

little

Without the serifs to guide the eye along the line, the strong verticals lead the eye downwards, against the natural reading direction.

Sans serif typefaces can work very well for headlines, where there are fewer words than in body text. They also work better on the web or in any digital medium, because they are easier to render out of the little square building blocks called pixels that make up on-screen images and text. They are cleaner and sharper and therefore easier to read.

If your house style dictates a sans serif face, don't despair. They aren't impossible to read. It's just that they are harder. You need to be aware of this and perhaps consider the overall effect of your typography.

Blocks and barriers

It's not enough to get the headline scheme, the point size and the typeface right. You have to think of the setting of the text overall. You have to avoid things that get in the way of easy reading and understanding. Below are some examples of what I mean.

Justified, ranged right, centred, reversed out and silly shaped text

If you want to make text in your business document as easy as possible to read, the best arrangement is ranged left, ragged right. All that means is a straight left-hand margin and a wiggly right-hand one.

Like this:
Sans serif typefaces can work very well for headlines, where there are fewer words than in body text. They also work better on the web or in any digital medium, because they are easier to render out of the little square building blocks called pixels that make up on-screen images and text. They are cleaner and sharper and therefore easier to read.

Justified text forces straight margins left and right. Like this:
Sans serif typefaces can work very well for headlines, where there are fewer words than in body text. They also work better on the web or in any digital medium, because they are easier to render out of the little square building blocks called pixels that make up on-screen images and text. They are cleaner and sharper and therefore easier to read.

Here, you tend to get rivers of white space snaking downwards through the text where your computer has forced extra word spacing to achieve the straight margins. These rivers lead the eye downwards when it should be running along the lines.

Centred text like this …
Sans serif typefaces can work very well for headlines, where there are fewer words than in body text. They also work better on the web or in any digital medium, because they are easier to render out of the little square building blocks called pixels that make up on-screen images and text. They are cleaner and sharper and therefore easier to read.

… can look attractive, but the eye has to come back to a new starting point for every line. This is tiring and there is a risk that your reader will miss a start point and skip a line or two.

Ranged right, like this …
Sans serif typefaces can work very well for headlines, where there are fewer words than in body text. They also work better on the web or in any digital medium, because they are easier to render out of the little square building blocks called pixels that make up on-screen images and text. They are cleaner and sharper and therefore easier to read.

… causes the same problem as centring. It also looks back to front.

And reversed-out text, like this …

Sans serif typefaces can work very well for headlines, where there are fewer words than in body text. They also work better on the web or in any digital medium, because they are easier to render out of the little square building blocks called pixels that make up on-screen images and text. They are cleaner and sharper and therefore easier to read.

… is almost asking your reader NOT to make the effort. Because effort is what they'll need to read this text. We learn to read black words on a white ground. Our daily newspapers and all our books are set this way. So turning convention on its head is asking for trouble.

The exception is text that people have to read in the dark. So if you are writing theatre programmes or slides for a dark auditorium, go with white text on a dark ground.

Setting text in silly shapes, like this …

Sans serif
typefaces can work very
well for headlines, where there are fewer
words than in body text. They also
work better on the web or in
any digital medium,
because they are
easier to
render
out
of the
little square
building blocks
called pixels that
make up on-screen image.

… is just ridiculous. (But people still do it.)

Broken bulleted lists

Bullet points are an excellent way of breaking up long narrative copy and highlighting key points. Just make sure all the bullets lie underneath the heading. Never break a bulleted list over a column. You're left with a few straggling orphans (single words or short lines) hanging around at the top of the next column. It's far better either to reduce the list until it fits comfortably in the space available, or to redesign the page so the whole list is kept together.

Overlong paragraphs

Strictly speaking, a paragraph is a unit of thought, not of length. That is to say, it isn't over till it's over. You keep going until you have expressed the idea or thought completely. Unfortunately, this may result in long and forbidding slabs that are visually offputting to your reader.

It pays to break up paragraphs once they reach five or six lines. Or two or three on the web. Now, this is, of course, an arbitrary limit, and your own judgement will tell you whether your copy is looking dull. But leaving thoughts incomplete has a very positive effect on readership. It forces people to move on to the next paragraph. Why?

Because, as we saw in Chapter 13, it taps a basic human need—the need for completion. I just did it there, ending the last paragraph with "why".

Once you acquire this skill, you can manipulate your reader subtly, encouraging them along with well-placed questions, dangling ideas and promised payoffs.

Poor colour mixes

As I've said, the most effective colour combination for maximum readability is black on white. An upmarket version of this is dark blue or dark grey on cream.

Yellow or pale grey type on a white background is virtually impossible to read (and I have seen both used), while certain combinations, red on green, for example, jitter together and won't stand still long enough to be read.

Chapter 23
Design—what designers can do (and what you should never allow them to)

A good designer can make the difference between a sale and no sale. They can apply their knowledge of, and feel for, typography, white space, navigation and colour to increase the impact of your copy and ensure your reader gets the message loud and clear.

The best designer I have ever worked with (still do, daily, as a matter of fact) is Ross Speirs of Colophon, in Oxfordshire. Ross and I have collaborated for over 15 years on everything from mailshots for the British Standards Institution to ads for *Practical Caravan* magazine.

He does something unusual among designers. He reads my copy. And this is one of the good things designers can do for you. By reading your copy they can see important messages—maybe even sentences or phrases that need highlighting—and pull them out as headlines, quotes or straplines.

Ross ensures my copy is as readable as possible. That's his goal. (He asks what the piece is for, another rarity.) I wanted to get his take on good design, so I emailed him a handful of questions. Here are his replies:

Andy   Why should people hire a designer?
Ross   For the same reason people hire a carpenter or an electrician. A designer worth the fee will have a wealth of experience in the detailed crafting of type and graphic elements into coherent and legible

marketing literature—a level of expertise that takes years to acquire. The DIY enthusiast is usually betrayed in the detail.

A What should a copywriter look for in a designer?

R Experience relevant to the project in hand. A grasp of the importance of words, of narrative, and of clear, well-structured copy. A full understanding of the function and objective of the piece—how it will be received, who will be reading it, what response you want.

A How does a good designer help the copywriter achieve their goals?

R By reading and understanding the copy. Good copy will give a good designer the lead and cues required to give the words life on the page. A good designer can bring graphic experience to bear on the structure and detail of the narrative.

A What's the single biggest thing a good designer can do with text?

R Make it legible.

A How can you tell if you've been given some good design?

R You should hardly notice it. The message should come through (on all levels) swiftly, clearly, without impediment.

A What's the most important question you should ask a designer before giving them any work?

R How much repeat business do you get from clients?

Never let your designer do any of this …

As copywriters, we spend (or ought to) many hours of our lives at the pixel-face, chipping diamonds out of the rock. So why are so many of us content to hock our words to art directors and web graphic designers whose main aim in life seems to be to produce something "cool"?

Remember, the designer is working for you, not the other way round. Given them a written brief. Even if you don't, refuse to accept they have a licence to indulge their high-art fantasies or trendy ideas on your hardworking sales materials.

I'm fortunate. Most of the time I get to work with a truly inspired—and inspiring—designer who understands that copy and design have to work together if we're going to achieve the results the client is looking for. But sometimes I have to get a sample brochure or letter designed by someone else. And you know what? Nine times out of ten it makes me weep.

There are lots of ways designers can screw up a perfectly good— even great—piece of sales copy. Here are three particularly offensive ones:

1   Hard-to-complete order forms
This might seem like a funny place to start, but I'm obsessed by order forms. Why? Oh, I don't know—maybe because that's how we get MONEY.

My bugbear is the designer who either lacks the skill to create something easy to complete, or exists on too elevated a plane to have to worry about whether anyone responds to their mailing piece. Apparently it's "cutting edge" to have the credit card boxes rendered as minuscule circles. And it's "cool" to require the reader to cut out an octopus-shaped coupon from a press ad. But we don't want what's cutting edge and what's cool at the expense of what works.

My tip? Boxes big enough for the average scrawler to write inside. Simple coupons that require two cuts at most.

2   Crap typography
Here's a little-known fact. It's little-known among the graphic design fraternity anyway. Ready?

As people get older, their eyesight gets worse.

So setting copy in seven- or eight-point type poses a real challenge to most of your customers. Especially on the web, or when combined with poor-contrast colours or white text over colour photographs or text backgrounds (no, I don't know why this is supposed to be a good idea either).

Also to be reviled are corporate style guides (usually produced at vast expense and ignored within a week of their thumping onto everybody's desks) that stipulate ridiculous typographical arrangements like justifying all text or using sans serif faces for all body copy, no matter how small.

My tip? Use a point size people can read without reaching for their reading glasses. And ignore the corporate ID department's strictures on typography. (Unless they're any good. Which they frequently aren't.)

3   Meaningless imagery

A man stands in a beautifully appointed office. There are no sheets of paper in sight. He lifts a slat in the Venetian blind and peers down at the ant-like workers on the street below. He sucks the end of his designer spectacles while speaking into a sleek black mobile phone, laughing handsomely and pointing at a laptop screen. (He has many arms.)

He is advertising pensions. No, courier services. No, shirts. Software. Swimming trunks. I don't, in fact, know, because there are roughly 82,000 campaigns running right now with that image.

My tip? Show your customer what you expect them to buy. Commission original photography. Hurt the next person who brings you an ad layout with a smiley executive in it. (Unless you sell smiley executives.)

Summary

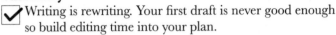Writing is rewriting. Your first draft is never good enough so build editing time into your plan.

It's essential that you proof-read everything. That includes emails. Proof-read your work on paper not on screen.

Get into the habit of checking readability statistics—and aiming for higher scores.

Look on layout and typography as two more copywriting tools. Used intelligently, they can dramatically increase the impact of your words.

Make sure your designer understands the purpose of your writing. Ensure they only do things that help your reader make sense of and respond to the text.

Section Six

What now?

"They say that nobody is perfect.
Then they tell you practice makes perfect.
I wish they'd make up their minds."

Winston Churchill, writer and

British Prime Minister, 1874—1965

Chapter 24
My tips for action . . .

This book contains some of the ideas, opinions and techniques that have sustained me as a copywriter since I started out. Get to know them, practise them, experiment with them and you'll become a better copywriter. The key word is "practise". Writing—even copywriting—can be pleasurable, but in the same way that gardening or playing the piano are pleasurable: you have to do some work. In this chapter, I want to give you a few pointers on how you can strengthen your skills as a copywriter.

Read—lots
Dr Johnson, that famous and oft-quoted expert on the English language, once said that an amateur is someone who writes more than he reads. What he meant is that to become a good writer, you need to study what other good writers do. The mere act of reading good writing will feed your own skill. It's almost as if you absorb good writing through your pores.

So the next question is, what do you read? It doesn't matter too much, as long as you read widely and choose good writers. I'd recommend the following though, just to get you started:

Magazines
The Economist—world-renowned for its analysis and clear writing.
The New Yorker—full of beautifully written articles, slightly freer and less business-y style than *The Economist*.

Newspapers
Any broadsheet, but if you really want to see crisp, punchy straightforward English, it has to be the *Sun*. Many people turn their noses up at this paper, but its writing is peerless (and grammatically correct).

For sheer mastery of the long, complex sentence and esoteric vocabulary you should read a copy of the *Times Literary Supplement*. I can't promise that you'll understand every word, but this is undoubtedly fine writing.

Writers on writing

Too many to compile a definitive list but my heroes include David Ogilvy, Drayton Bird, Claude Hopkins, Walter Weintz and Robert Bly from the world of copywriting, and Stephen King and Ursula LeGuin from the world of fiction.

Fiction

Your own tastes are far more important than mine. But why not choose an author, genre, or period you normally avoid, just to see what you can pick up? And who knows, you might find you enjoy it. My favourites include Charles Dickens, Anthony Trollope, Jane Austen, John Updike, Jonathan Safran Foer, George Saunders, Philip Roth, Robertson Davies, Margaret Atwood, Raymond Carver, Joyce Carol Oates, Ian McEwan, William Trevor, Muriel Spark and Peter Carey.

Business writing

I hesitate to recommend business writing for examples of how to do it right, since much, if not most, of it is more a lesson in what not to do. But … read the reports, emails, mailshots and proposals you receive with a critical eye as well as a business one and you'll start to see the good as well as the bad.

And if you see a phrase or a word or a way of structuring copy that you like, don't be afraid to steal it. All professional writers occasionally take this magpie approach to writing.

"Lady, you gotta practise"

A little old lady stops by a construction site on Fifth Avenue in New York and says to the workman, "Excuse me young man, how do I get to Carnegie Hall?" And the workman says, "Lady, you gotta practise."

That goes for writing, too. And with respect to the venerable Dr J, you'll never be more than an amateur unless you practise your writing. But what is practising? Does it just mean writing lots? Or is there something more active we can do? It's a bit of both, really. First though, you need to become aware of what you are doing as you write.

Most of us spend our careers bashing out copy without ever really thinking about what we're doing. We are just too busy trying to get it finished and sent to consider such things as word choice, word order, punctuation or tone of voice. But they count. Here are a few guidelines on practising.

1   To be able to practise, you need to become aware of your writing as writing. You need to see it as others see it. The best way I have found is to print it out (whatever it is) and leave it overnight. Now, I know that deadlines and the hectic pace of your job mean that won't be possible for everything you write, but when you have a slightly longer lead time, try it.

When you come back to it, read it carefully and look at it from a critical perspective, using the issues in this book as triggers. How is it punctuated? How long are the sentences and paragraphs? Does it flow? Is it clear and unambiguous?

2   Take some recent copy you've written and see how much shorter you can make it without losing any of the really important points. You'll be surprised.

3   Get yourself a writing buddy and swap a piece of work with them. Write a short critique explaining what you like, and why, and what you don't like, and why. Then swap back and explain how you arrived at your comments.

4   For the next piece of copy you have to write, make a plan and stick to it. Remember, time spent planning is saved many times over later on. See how much easier it is to write copy when you are free to concentrate on the writing because the content is already determined.

5   Check the readability statistics on each new piece of copy you write and then recheck as you write further drafts. Get it right and your scores should improve. This will show you how specific things you do improve readability.

6   Copy out passages of copywriting that you think work, that have made you respond with an order, or that you have found in manuals or handbooks on copywriting. This process links your hand, eye and brain to those of an expert: it works and it's been used down the centuries by many of the world's greatest writers to improve their own style. You'll see artists doing exactly the same thing, sitting in galleries copying Old Masters.

Chapter 25
How to brief an external copywriter

With the tips and techniques in *Write to Sell*, you have all you need to start writing better sales copy. Except for one thing. Time. You're a busy person. You're running an account, a process or function, a team, a department, a business. That's a lot of items on your to do list. I only have one on mine: writing.

There will be times when you need, and hopefully want, to do your own copywriting. But when you want a fresh pair of eyes, or simply another pair of hands, you need an external copywriter. And when you do, the good ones will ask you for a brief, preferably a written brief.

So what, exactly, is a brief?
In essence, a brief tells the external copywriter about you, your company, your product and, most importantly, your customers or prospects. It should tell them what you want to achieve. It should not, ideally, tell them how to do it. That's their job. After all, you wouldn't buy a dog and bark yourself. (Or would you? Some clients seem to take a perverse delight in hiring a copywriter—and then telling them not just what to write and how but, finally, rewriting their copy altogether.)

A key function of the brief is to act as a written record of what you have asked for. It forms, in other words, the basis of the contract between you and your copywriter. If what you get back doesn't match the brief, you have grounds for asking for a rewrite. If it does, but you just don't like the style, then you are into negotiation territory. Any good copywriter should be happy to redraft something if you're not happy with the tone or style, provided you haven't changed the brief since commissioning the work.

Do you have to meet?

You don't have to meet: I have clients in New York, Vienna, Brussels and Hong Kong whom I have never met. We all have phones, Skype, email, videoconferencing if we want them. But it's nice to meet. After all, one of the theses of this book is that we are all human. And it's a natural human desire to meet the people with whom we do business.

If you do meet, make sure there's an agreed agenda. Don't waste your time (or theirs) with a rambling, unfocused chat.

What goes into the brief?

You can put into your brief anything you like. It should all, though, help your copywriter understand the buying chain, from the product to the client. If they are any good at all they will ask you lots of questions. Here is the outline of a standard questionnaire I use with clients to help them focus. Please feel free to adapt this for your own needs. Numbers 10 to 16 will only be relevant if you're handling design and print, too.

Sunfish marketing brief

Client:
Client contact:
Campaign/product name:
Target completion date:
Summary of creative requirements:
Enclosures:

1   About the reader—please supply as much detail as possible about the target reader of the copy, eg demographic and professional profiles. Plus try to answer these questions:

- What keeps them awake at 3am?
- What are they hungry for?
- What do they want less of?
- What will happen if they do what you want?

- What won't happen if they do what you want?
- What will happen if they don't do what you want?
- What won't happen if they don't do what you want?

2 Overall campaign objectives Ultimate goal, eg generate enquiries or sales, inform prospects and clients, build brand recognition and preference, recapture previous purchasers etc. What do you want the reader to know, feel and commit?

3 Product information Type of product, product/brand names, content etc.

4 Unique selling proposition What are the special characteristics of this product that make it better than the competition? What are its strengths (and weaknesses if any)?

5 How does it benefit the purchaser? How is their life improved by buying the product? What's in it for them?

6 Strategy How will you achieve your goal? Type of campaign being launched and why? Communications channels—online, offline, combination?

7 Lists/target media Mailing list selections, in-house databases, magazines, newspapers etc.

8 Schedule When do you need the first draft; when do you need final copy and final artwork?

9 Company's core values/positioning What sort of image are we trying to convey, eg serious and authoritative, fun and funky, upmarket and reserved, friendly and reliable … any combination of these or other values?

10 Visuals/concept work Do you want visuals/alternative creative treatments before copy goes into design stage? How many ideas?

11 Typography Are there any specific typefaces that we must include or exclude? Are there any specific typographical rules/editorial guidelines (eg house style) that form part of your marketing or corporate policy?

12 Colour How many colours are we to use? Are there any particular colours that we must include or avoid? Are there any ways in which you want to use colour (eg solid ground on front cover, large blocks of solid colour, tints)?

13 Layout and format Is there a specific required format for printed documents (eg 4pp A4, 8pp A5, 6pp DL)? What size envelope will you use if it is to be mailed? Is there a specific feel we are trying to create (eg busy, spacious, relaxed)?

14 Logos and graphics Are there any specific graphic elements which we must include (eg logos, screen dumps, graphics, illustrations, photos)? How many and where will they come from (eg Sunfish to provide, client to provide)?

15 Software What software package is preferred by/ acceptable to your printer?

16 Other issues Any other important notes on house style or creative aspects?

Dealing with corrections

Over the past couple of decades, I have written a great deal of copy. For the first ten, while I was working in-house, nobody ever said they liked my work, or offered any praise. (Boo hoo, poor me.) As soon as I started working as an independent copywriter, the praise started flowing. Why is this? Maybe people respect the craftsmen they hire but not their own employees, I don't know. But here's my point.

When you get your first draft back from your copywriter, they will be feeling anxious. They'll hope that you like it, and, by extension, them. They'll worry that you won't. They've put a lot of time and effort into this first draft and they desperately need a little stroke before hearing the bad news (if there is any).

If you want to build a solid working relationship with your external copywriter, therefore, I recommend that you find something positive to say to start with. They'll be pathetically grateful and you can then lead them gently into the areas where you feel a little more work is needed.

Be aware, too, that there are two basic categories of amendments. The first are those changes you want made because the copywriter hasn't grasped your product, company, customer or selling points. That's their fault and they should put it right at no extra charge.

The second are those changes you want made because, for example, you have changed your mind about some aspect of the campaign or sales piece while they were off writing the first draft. They should still be willing to make these changes but you should, in turn, be willing to pay for the additional work. We're back to the brief. If it's not on the brief, you can't expect them to have incorporated it into the copy.

Chapter 26
The last word

People have been predicting the death of the written word for some time now. The telephone was supposed to wound it. The Internet was supposed to kill it. And mobiles were supposed to feast on its carcass. What happened? The reverse. There are more written words now than ever.

Catch a train these days and your neighbour is more likely to be typing than reading. Attend a meeting and at least one of the participants is probably sending emails from their BlackBerry. Switch your mobile phone on and see how many texts you've received in the past few hours.

Why good writing matters
Although I didn't come out with it at the beginning, one of my aims in writing this book was to help you write better English, full stop.

Yes, I want you to run a more profitable business. Yes, I want your brochures, ads, websites and emails to be more effective. But I also want to see a world in which copywriting can hold its head up in polite company. That won't happen as long as we are prepared to tolerate the lurching, badly stitched-together "communications" that too many companies seem happy to churn out.

Every time a company sends out a badly written press release, or an email containing spelling and punctuation errors, or a brochure stuffed with clichés, the English language suffers another insult. They're hard to repair, too. i-Literate Ltd's chimp-written mailer goes to two or three million people. Maybe they think i-Literate, Ltd knows what it's doing and assume that goes for its use of English. Maybe they start using the same rubbishy language. Maybe their children see it and they start copying it as well. Not good.

The truth is, good writing will always be more effective than bad, whether it's used for love letters or sales letters. Your writing should always be pleasurable to read, even if it's employed "merely" for selling things.

Get it right and you'll gain improved business results, of course. But you'll also derive personal pride, pleasure and satisfaction, as I do, from crafting elegant, fresh and compelling sales messages in English.

Summary

-  Become a better copywriter by reading as much and as widely as you can.

- 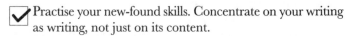 Practise your new-found skills. Concentrate on your writing as writing, not just on its content.

- 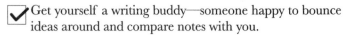 Get yourself a writing buddy—someone happy to bounce ideas around and compare notes with you.

- 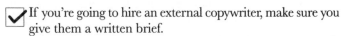 If you're going to hire an external copywriter, make sure you give them a written brief.

- Remember, writers need the good news first.

- Shakespeare used English too, so we should treat it with respect.

Appendix 1
Writing for the web—myths and realities

Introduction

There are plenty of self-proclaimed experts who will tell you that online copywriting is a brave new world. It has nothing to do with offline copywriting (that's print, by the way). It is a completely new discipline. And then they tell you that every web page needs a headline. The truth is, there ARE differences between online and offline copywriting. But these are fewer than many suppose. We are still trying to do the same things we have always tried to do: persuade people to open, read, believe and act on our copy.

The Internet has changed things. But not in the way most people think. It doesn't mean copy matters less. (In fact, it matters more.) Nor has it changed the way people respond to copy. What the internet has done is increase the amount of rubbish directed at consumers and businesspeople. It has given the illiterate, the irrelevant and the idiotic equal billing with your carefully crafted marketing campaigns. Which means simply, this. Copywriting in the digital age is *harder*.

What are the myths?

Just as with any new technology, there are plenty of people with a vested interest in creating myths … they want you to feel bewildered so you pay them vast sums of money as "consultants". Here are a few of the more common myths being peddled about online copywriting:

Myth #1 "Web and e-zine copy must be more information than promotion."

It has *never* been a good idea to make copy into a hard-sell, foot-in-the-door approach. Your customers want information to help them make a purchase decision, of course they do. And that's always been the case.

Myth #2 "Online copy must be scannable as well as easy to read word-for-word."

It's true that people scan web copy. But that goes for printed brochures, too. And ads, sales letters and flyers.

Myth #3 "Web users aren't always highly literate or fluent readers so you must always use simple text."

Again, there are people online who aren't fluent readers of English or even very literate. But they were there before, receiving your mailshots, reading your press advertising and looking at your posters. The question is, are these people part of your target market?

If they are then of course you need to keep it simple. But if you are writing for a sophisticated and highly educated audience, the myth vanishes.

Myth #4 "The web community is a global one, so you should avoid local idiom."

If you have a product and service that can be bought by everyone on the planet, this may apply to you. But if your copy is shorn of all local expressions and turns of phrase, it may also lose the very individuality that will make people want to do business with you.

Myth #5 "It's more important that you build trust on the web."

Why? Yes, there are scammers and spammers online so your web copy must stand head and shoulders above theirs in positioning you as a trustworthy vendor. But wasn't that always true? Those conmen (and women) weren't doing nothing until the advent of the web, remember. People have *never* bought from people they didn't trust.

Everything starts with the headline

On the web, where readers feel they have less time to "get" what a piece of copy is about, structure is all-important. It's your job to help your reader navigate your web page and find the information they're looking for as quickly as possible. But it's also important that you lead your reader where you want them to go. Usually to a buying decision of some sort.

The print formula AIDCA, which we covered in Chapter 10, works perfectly on the web. Just make sure you really grab their attention and never write about stuff that doesn't interest your reader. The thread holding their attention is thinner and more fragile than ever and is easily severed.

Imagine your reader looking at a page full of Google results. There are ten listed sites plus a similar number of Google Adwords on the right. What can you do to ensure the reader clicks onto your site? The answer is, grab their attention with a powerful headline. Because that's what these pieces of microtext are: headlines.

Now imagine that someone has arrived at your site. Maybe the home page, maybe not. Either way, they're looking for clues that staying will be beneficial to them. As they scan the page, the first thing they look at is the headline. And here's a huge practical tip: forget about writing "Welcome to …" at the top of your homepage. This lame excuse for a headline does nothing except lump your site in with the millions of other no-hopers using the same line.

Instead, give your reader a concrete reason to read on. Give them a benefit. Give them some news. Make them think. Get them curious about what you have to say. If you've created a list of seven benefits of subscribing to your property database, for example, you could just head the page:

Benefits

But it's ten times more powerful to involve the reader. Like this …

Seven property secrets revealed when you join us

Subject lines

Email subject lines are a special case. They are headlines. But their main function is to ensure your email gets opened. In this respect they are a lot like old-school envelope teaser lines. The difference is, they could be appearing in a list of dozens or hundreds of other lines. There are a few additional rules to follow when writing subject lines that pay massive dividends in terms of opening rates.

1   Put powerful keywords at the beginning. As people scan their inboxes, they often only really scan the first word of each subject line.

2   Avoid sounding like a spammer. The jury is still out on whether "free" automatically triggers spam filters. It has always been the marketer's secret weapon, so discard it only after careful testing.

3   Keep them short. Aim for 40 characters including spaces to avoid Outlook and other email clients truncating your subject line.

Online style and tone of voice

There aren't any words that are specific to the web, or to printed communications. And to a great extent, good online style mirrors good offline style. As great copywriters, particularly great direct mail copywriters, have known for decades, it's always a good idea to use short pithy words and sentences to connect with your reader.

Online, it makes sense to keep your sentences as short as possible. Aim for ten words on average. That's a tough target, but even if you miss it, your copy will be far more readable than most sites, which means your site will be stickier and more likely to persuade people to buy from you. And aim for a conversational tone of voice. The web is an informal medium, almost by definition, so you can afford to use a less formal register in your online copy than you would offline.

Length of copy

One of the biggest, and most persistent, myths surrounding online copy is that it has to be short. Evidence is rarely provided to support this assertion. The writers usually prefer vague statements such as, "people get tired reading online". Or, even less convincingly, "people won't read long copy on the web".

The trick is: keep it relevant. Focus unremittingly on your reader's interests, concerns, hopes, fears and motivations and they'll repay you with their attention. Learn from your offline cousins: test different lengths of copy and find the winning formula.

It's just possible that for your market and your products, short copy will outpull long. But you need to be sure before you lose out on the extra profits long copy could bring you.

Hypertext

Hypertext is an incredibly powerful tool for us as online copywriters (and even more so for our readers) because it allows us to create multiple paths through our copy. In other words, we can give our readers control of how they take in our information.

Rather than ploughing through a dense product brochure, they can zero in on just those facts and copy elements that THEY want to read before making their decision to buy.

Text links in body copy provide a less formal navigation system for web pages and allow the reader an alternative route to the navbar. And they actually play on both scanning and skimming reading strategies. Best of all, from your reader's perspective, they allow them to drill down to get more detailed information on the subjects that interest them.

You still write it the way you would for print, but you structure it using hypertext so the story unfolds on multiple levels: the basics for people who just want a quick read and the deeper-level information for the more interested—or sceptical—reader.

Conclusion

Almost all the points in this book apply to online copywriting as well as offline. But …

Whether you're writing an email, a web page or a banner ad, you have to fight to be heard above a mounting cacophony of badly written messages foisted on an unwilling readership by everyone from get-rich-quick hucksters to beady-eyed spammers. So you're under additional pressure to get it right.

Pay particular attention to your tone of voice—people reading emails or web pages are predisposed to accept a less formal approach. So as long as your copy is still in tune with your brand, you can afford to relax a little. And remember to check readability ruthlessly. I have seen many examples of web pages scoring 10% or less on the Flesch Reading Ease score (of which more in Chapter 21).

Finally, remember this. Good online copywriting must sell, first and foremost. The paradigm may have changed from promotion to education, but the underlying purpose remains unchanged.

Appendix 2
Copywriters' reference sources

There are hundreds of reference books on English usage, business
English and copywriting … thousands of ezines, websites and blogs.
It's fun to build your own reference shelf but here are the books on
my bookshelf:

Concise Oxford English Dictionary
(Oxford University Press, 2006)

The Economist Style Guide: The bestselling guide to English usage
(Profile Books, 2005)

Oxford Thesaurus of English
(Oxford University Press, 2006)

Drayton Bird, *Commonsense Direct Marketing*
(Kogan Page, 2000)

Drayton Bird, *How to Write Sales Letters
That Sell: Learn the secrets of successful direct mail*
(Kogan Page, 2002)

Robert W. Bly, *The Copywriter's Handbook:
A step-by-step guide to writing copy that sells*
(Owl Books, 2007)

Dorothea Brande, *Becoming a Writer*
(Jeremy P. Tarcher, 1981)

RW Burchfield, *Fowler's Modern English Usage*
(Oxford University Press, 2004)

John Caples, *Tested Advertising Methods*
(Prentice Hall, 1980)

GV Carey, *Mind the Stop: A brief guide to punctuation*
(Penguin Books, 1971)

Sylvia Chalker and Edmund Weiner,
The Oxford Dictionary of English Grammar
(Oxford Paperbacks, 1998)

James Cochrane, *Between You and I: A little book of bad English*
(Icon Books, 2005)

David Crystal, *The Cambridge Encyclopedia of the English Language*
(Cambridge University Press, 2003)

David Crystal, *The English Language: A guided tour of the language*
(Penguin Books, 2002)

Dianne Doubtfire and Ian Burton, *Teach Yourself Creative Writing*
(Teach Yourself Books, 2003)

John Fraser-Robinson, *The Secrets of Effective Direct Mail*
(McGraw-Hill Publishing, 1989)

Eric Gill, *An Essay on Typography*
(Theosophical University Press, 1993)

Sir Ernest Gowers, *Complete Plain Words:*
The classic desk companion for clear writing
(Penguin Books, 1987)

Claude C Hopkins, *My Life in Advertising & Scientific Advertising*
(McGraw-Hill, 1986)

John Humphrys, *Lost for Words:*
The mangling and manipulation of the English language
(Hodder and Stoughton Paperbacks, 2005)

Graham King, *Punctuation*
(Collins, 2000)

Stephen King, *On Writing: A memoir*
(New English Library, 2001)

Damon Knight, *Creating Short Fiction:*
The classic guide to writing short fiction
(St Martin's Press, 1997)

Elizabeth Knowles, *The Oxford Dictionary of 20th Century Quotations*
(Oxford University Press, 1999)

Elizabeth Knowles, *Oxford Dictionary of Quotations:*
The favourite guide to wit and wisdom past and present
(Oxford University Press, 2004)

Ursula K Le Guin, *Steering the Craft: Exercises and discussions*
on story writing for the lone navigator or the mutinous crew
(Eighth Mountain Press, 1999)

Graeme McCorkill, *Advertising That Pulls Response*
(McGraw-Hill Publishing, 1990)

David Ogilvy, *Confessions of an Advertising Man*
(Southbank Publishing, 2004)

David Ogilvy, *Ogilvy on Advertising*
(Random House, 1987)

David Ogilvy and Joel Raphaelson,
The Unpublished David Ogilvy: His secrets of management, creativity
and success – from private papers and public fulminations
(Crown, 1987)

David Oliver, *101 Ways to Negotiate More Effectively*
(Kogan Page, 1996)

Eric Partridge and Janet Whitcut,
Usage and Abusage: A guide to good English
(Penguin Books, 1999)

Flyn L Penoyer, *Teleselling Techniques That Close the Sale*
(Amacom, 1997)

Adrian Room, *Brewer's Dictionary of Phrase and Fable*
(Cassell, 2001)

Victor O Schwab, *How to Write a Good Advertisement*
(Wiltshire Book Company, 1985)

Sol Stein, *Solutions for Writers:*
Practical craft techniques for fiction and non-fiction
(Souvenir Press, 1999)

William Strunk, Jr and EB White, *The Elements of Style*
(Longman, 1999)

Alan Swann, *Basic Design and Layout: Principles and techniques
of graphic design demonstrated in step by step projects*
(Phaidon Press, 1987)

Lynne Truss, *Eats, Shoots and Leaves:
The zero tolerance approach to punctuation*
(Profile Books, 2005)

Jan Tschichold, *The Form of the Book: Essays on the morality of good design*
(Hartley and Marks, 2006)

Nick Usborne, *Net Words: Creating high-impact online copy*
(McGraw-Hill, 2001)

ESC Weiner and Andrew Delahunty, *The Oxford Guide
to English Usage: The essential guide to correct English*
(Oxford University Press, 1994)

Appendix 3
A note on the readability statistics for this book

When I finished the first draft of the first edition of *Write to Sell*, I ran the readability statistics. Here are my scores:

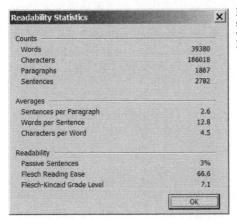

Microsoft product screen shot reprinted with permission from Microsoft Corporation.

Look at those great ratios. My sentences usually contain around 13 words—well inside the limit for the average reader's understanding (and I know, dear reader, that you are anything but average).

Just 3 per cent of the 2,782 sentences in this book are in the passive voice.

My Flesch Reading Ease score is a very respectable 66.6—above the magic number 60, where plain English starts.

And my Flesch-Kincaid Grade Level is 7.1, that is, it's understandable to someone with a reading age of 12.1.

Acknowledgements

I couldn't have written *Write to Sell* without the experience I've gained working for clients all over the world.

Several people generously took time to read the book in its early stages and give me invaluable feedback. Sally Bibb of The Economist Group encouraged me to stop procrastinating and start writing. Ross Speirs, another friend and a designer of inestimable talent, helped particularly with the sections on design. Jo Maslen, my wife and commercial director of Sunfish, has provided wise counsel since I set up the agency: that extended to this book.

Scott Keyser, my partner in our training venture, Write for Results, helped me shape my thoughts on what matters in business writing.

Martin Liu, Pom Somkabcharti and the team at Marshall Cavendish are wonderful to work with. I have gained immeasurably by listening to their sound advice about book publishing.

Finally, two figures from the world of advertising and direct marketing whose own books have provided a constant source of inspiration: David Ogilvy and Drayton Bird.

Thank you all.